LET'S MAKE A MEMORY

Gloria Gaither *and* Shirley Dobson

Great Ideas for Building Family Traditions and Togetherness

Illustrations by Russ Flint

WORD BOOKS
PUBLISHER
WACO, TEXAS
A DIVISION OF
WORD, INCORPORATED

*This book is
affectionately dedicated to
our husbands, Jim Dobson and Bill Gaither,
and to the Dobson children, Danae and Ryan, and
the Gaither children, Suzanne, Amy, and Benjy,
with whom we share lifetimes
of priceless memories.*

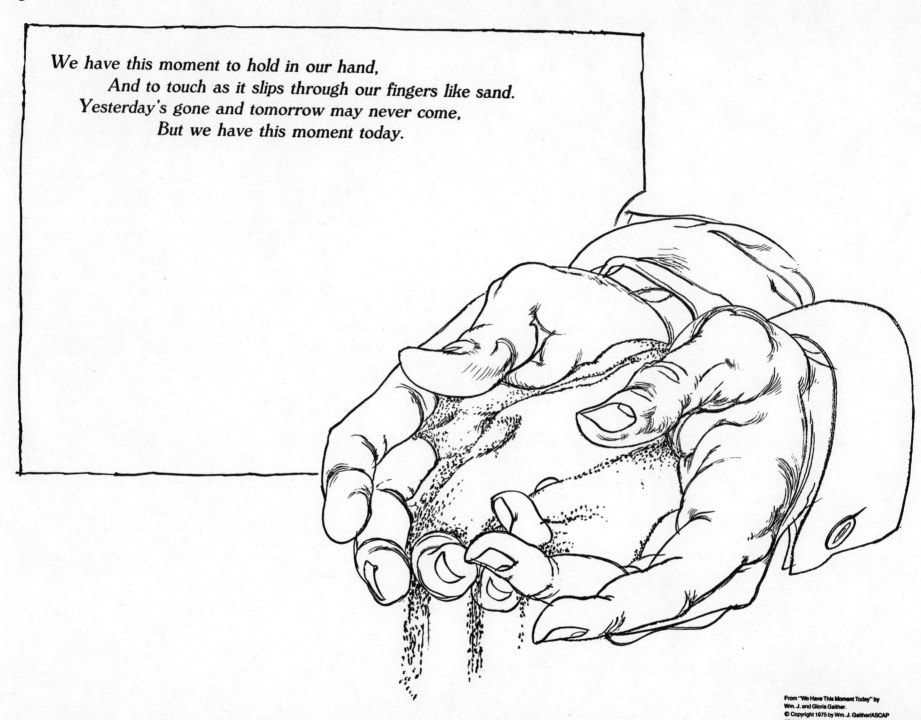

We have this moment to hold in our hand,
    And to touch as it slips through our fingers like sand.
Yesterday's gone and tomorrow may never come,
    But we have this moment today.

ACKNOWLEDGMENTS

Originality is the art of concealing your source, it is said, for there is no creative effort that does not draw on the inspiration we glean from one another. In this instance, however, we wish not to conceal—but to acknowledge—the sources that have contributed generously to the writing of this book. We are grateful to the following individuals for sharing their family traditions with us:

Joyce Landorf, the Millard Posthuma family, Joy MacKenzie, Joe Bayly, and all others whose contributions appear in the Memorable Memory Makers section of this book.

Also, we are indebted to others who encouraged and assisted us in immeasurable ways, including:

Jan Starks, Flo Waltrip, Phyllis Esler, Dee Otte, Helen Kolodny, Pat Wienandt, project managing editor; Beth Maybee, assistant editor; Merle Oliver, manuscript typist; Janice Gibson, finished art specialist; Dennis Hill, art director; Ronald Garman, project designer and Russ Flint, illustrator, for the outstanding artwork.

These are the individuals for whom the greatest appreciation and love are due. But there is a larger body of contributors whom we *cannot* acknowledge personally. They represent the great host of unidentified conveyors of folk wisdom, crafts projects, and traditions that we've included in this book. We simply do not *know* where each of the ideas originated. They have become part of the culture in which we live. That is, in fact, the purpose for our book—to expand and vitalize those activities that give identity and meaning to the loving relationships within the context of today's families.

CONTENTS

GLORIA'S STORY

In my life I have been given many wonderful gifts: lovely handmade embroidered items, expensive works of art, earthy rustic crafts, primitive water paintings on simple newsprint created by the chubby little hands of children. I have been honored and complimented. I have had the thrill of hearing the songs I've helped to create recorded by famous singers and sung by congregations in my own and foreign languages. These are all gifts I treasure.

But none of these gifts has been so valuable to me as the gift of a rich childhood and youth in a solid, loving, celebrating home. The heritage of a family who loved God and each other, who greeted every new day with anticipation and openness, shaped my values and taught me that life was good. The healthy balance of discipline and freedom, the love

of simple things, the respect for all kinds of persons, a deep reverence for God—all these were wrapped up in special moments and given to me in the package I call my childhood.

I truly believe that most of what I've been able to do with my life has been a direct result of the rich heritage I enjoyed. I am certain that my family gave me a head start on life with a realistic concept of God and His Son, a love affair with nature, and an excitement for living. My home brought me to the threshold of adulthood with a secure confidence that I was loved and a deep responsibility to myself and the world around me for developing whatever special abilities and gifts God had given me.

My parents always pastored small Michigan churches, so we never traveled widely or were afforded the luxuries some families enjoy. Instead, we learned to celebrate life in simple ways and to create our own special moments and traditions from the raw material of common things. My mother, who was an ártist and writer, taught my sister and me to see what many others missed. She gave us a deep appreciation for beauty and books and a great love for words and language. Daddy was the master of spur-of-the-moment parties on a shoe string: a Dairy Queen after church, a roadside picnic breakfast, the presentation of a special dress he'd scrimped to buy for Mother for an important event. It was Daddy who gave me my very own garden spot (even though he had to dig up the thick, green sod to do it) and gave me full rein to plant *anything* I wanted to. I learned from him the joy of "preferring one another," as every summer we would take fishing trips to the far north because Mother loved to fish. I remember him digging fishing worms, cleaning bass and catfish until midnight, lugging soggy rowboats into and out of the lakes, and rowing for miles, all just because he loved seeing Mother get so much fun out of "hooking a big one."

At our house everything was an event, and it was to our house that Evelyn's and my friends always came to "hang out"; we knew that if we needed a place for a gathering of any kind, it was okay to volunteer our place. Mother was the confidante for many a teenager, and it was not uncommon for someone in distress to knock on our door at midnight seeking comfort and advice. It never occurred to me to keep anything from her. She was and is my best friend. Now our own children run to her house when they need someone to talk to or simply a place to be. Just now, she is teaching our son to paint with oils and to see things in the world around him that others miss. She is critiquing our daughters' poetry and boyfriends. She is their friend.

When I married Bill, I found another big, loving family—an Indiana farm family, who loved the earth and celebrated harvests and holidays, Sundays and birthdays with big dinners and warm family gatherings: tables groaning with home-grown vegetables, fresh corn-fed meat, and steaming fruit desserts; children of all ages and sizes scampering around the patriarchs and assorted distant relations; the joyous noise of adult conversation, shrieking children, and spontaneous music.

Because we so appreciate our own heritages, Bill and I have chosen to live near both our families. We feel there is great value for our children in knowing their roots that gives them a sense of perspective and continuity. In a society as mobile as the one we all live in, Bill and I feel very blessed that we've been able to offer our children a close relationship with their extended family and close friendships with their young cousins and aging relatives. Living close to our extended family has not always been problem free, but we feel the benefits far outweigh any problems. Good or bad, family is family and life is life. We feel children need a realistic view of the influences that have come together to make up the sum total of what they are.

Now that Bill and I, Suzanne, Amy, and Benjy have come to be a family ourselves, we draw from the rich heritage we have been given. Daily we work upon this base to build the kind of family we believe God wants us to be. Together we are learning to care more, love more unselfishly, and reach into our community with compassion. We know that each of us is still a "kid under construction" and as children of God, we must help one another become what God wants each to be. Some days it is Amy who helps me to grow; other days Bill lifts Suzanne. At times, Benjy is a great teacher for us all. Together we are growing in the soil of our home, fed and nourished by the nutrients of our shared pasts, from the seeds God has planted in us.

It is in gratitude and to celebrate our heritage that I have worked with Shirley to create this book. Both of us, from our very different perspectives, believe that the family must be the basic spiritual, moral, educational, and physical unit of our society or we will have no society.

We believe that special moments don't *just happen*; they have to be planned *on purpose!* In this hectic world when the pace at which we all live is so frantic, we as families must make a covenant with each other to make time for simple things. Please hear me now! *Special moments won't just happen.* Beautiful memories of yesterdays were once moments of todays. We have no guarantees of tomorrows, but we do have this moment.

The home is the natural habitat for growing human beings and shaping eternal souls. Whether we like it or not, we are molding lives . . . now. Let's make these precious moments count. Let's make a memory!

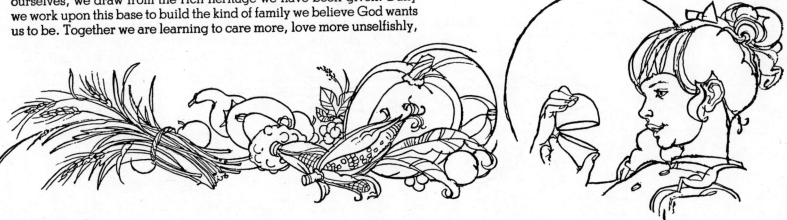

SHIRLEY'S STORY

I see a little girl skipping home from school in the late afternoon sun. Her dress is a hand-me-down, intended for someone two sizes larger. Her shoes are unpolished and her socks no longer have elastic around the top. She reaches her destination and walks across a barren yard toward a small house. It is badly in need of paint and repair, but the mother who lives there can barely afford to feed and clothe her son and daughter.

How tenderly I feel for this little child of poverty. It is almost as though she were my own daughter, and I ache to hold her in my arms . . . to buy her a pretty new dress . . . to give her a shiny new bicycle. But that is impossible—for we are separated by three decades of time. I can neither talk to her nor meet her needs. For that little girl, you see, is the memory of my own childhood. I walked in her shoes. I lived in that small unpainted house. And I can still feel the indescribable yearning of a child who knew that something vital was missing from her life.

I was the daughter of a confirmed alcoholic. Only those who have lived through this nightmare will understand the full implication of this experience. I could never ask a friend to spend the night for fear my father would return in a drunken stupor and embarrass me. Night after night, he would stumble home in the early morning hours, belligerent and foul-mouthed. We would be awakened by his shouting and threats and would often hide to avoid his wrath. The rooms of our home had been patched with brown butcher paper and painted over to conceal where he had shoved his fists through the walls in fits of anger.

Like other children of an alcoholic parent, I learned to hide my disgrace. I remember being driven home from a birthday party on one occasion, and asking to be left at a clean house with a well-manicured yard. I

waved goodbye and marched up the driveway as if it were my own, but when the car rounded the corner, I turned and walked several blocks to my house.

It was only through the wisdom and devotion of my mother that I survived the emotional pressures of those years. She is a strong woman, and she marshaled all of her resources to hold our little family together. Since Dad spent his entire paycheck at the bar each Friday night, Mother went to work to support the family. She found a job at a fish cannery which required her to work unpredictable hours. Many times she would be called at three or four in the morning after having been kept awake all night by her harassing, drunken husband. I marveled at her ability to hold a job and to do the marketing, cooking, housekeeping, and laundry under those stressful circumstances.

Most importantly, Mom convinced my brother and me that she loved us. And because of that love, she constantly sought ways to get us through those difficult years. She had the wisdom to know that she needed help in raising two rambunctious kids, and she turned for assistance to a local evangelical church. Mom would not go with us (Sunday was her "catch up" day), but she insisted that we get involved. She would pull back the blankets every Sunday morning and order us to get ready for church. We complained and moaned, but to no avail. Mom was not a practicing Christian, but she knew that churches offered more than one kind of "salvation," and her children needed all the help they could get.

It was in that little neighborhood church that I was introduced to Jesus Christ, and invited Him into my heart and life. He became my special friend, and I've never been the same since that moment. My pastor taught me that God cared about my personal concerns, so I began to pray for my home. My father continued to drink and associate with other women, so our situation grew steadily worse. Finally, in desperation, I went into my bedroom and cried out to God:

"If Dad isn't going to change, then please get us out of this house and give us the kind of father that will love and provide for us."

The Lord heard that prayer. After much suffering and agony involving Dad's continued drunkenness and an illicit relationship with a neighbor, my parents were divorced. I was in the sixth grade. We moved to a little shanty we called "our chicken coop," but for the first time, we could lie down in peace and enjoy an uninterrupted night's sleep.

My mother remarried a year later to a man who had been a confirmed bachelor. Joe was not a Christian at the time, but he was a man with high moral standards. We fell for his sunny disposition and big smile. He became a faithful husband and a good provider. Soon we moved to our first "real house," with bedrooms of our own and a front lawn with genuine grass and flowers. Later, both my mother and stepfather became beautiful Christians and remain committed to the faith today.

But there was another prayer that I sent toward heaven during those darkest days. As a ten-year-old girl, I began talking to God about the man I would eventually marry. I asked Him to send me a Christian husband when the time was right, and not to let me fall into the private hell that my mother had experienced. Without realizing it, of course, I was praying at that moment for an eleven-year-old boy who was a thousand miles away, growing up in a loving, stable home like the one in my dreams.

My high school years proved to be relatively tranquil and I began to think about college. I enrolled in a Christian school with the financial help of my stepfather, and graduated four years later. Toward the end of my sophomore year, I began dating a tall, blond Texan named Jim Dobson. It didn't take me long to decide that he was the man I had been praying for since I was ten years old. I'll never forget the evening Jim and I were sitting in his car near the girl's dormitory, discussing our future together. He had asked me to marry him and I accepted. He turned to me and said, "I can't explain why you had to experience so much pain in your early childhood, but there is something I want you to know. I hereby pledge myself to the task of making up for those days. I am going to do the best I can to make you happy."

Jim and I will celebrate our twenty-third anniversary later this month, and he has kept that youthful commitment. He has constructed my self-esteem as though he were a brick mason building a fortress. He convinced me that I am a worthy person . . . that his love for me is unconditional, and that God has a place for me in His grand scheme for the universe. Our love for one another has never wavered throughout these two decades of daily togetherness, which is a miracle in itself. There is no doubt that God answered the second tearful prayer of a little girl named Shirley.

He has also blessed us with two healthy, energetic children and a lovely home. There are times when I stand and gaze at His gifts and find it difficult to realize that I am the recipient of them. Of course, to be honest, there have been difficult moments in our adult lives. We've experienced our share of reverses and sad times and illnesses. During the past three years, for example, we've lost eight members of our small family in death. But even during these times of tragedy, the presence of God has been evident to each of us. We will, after all, be united on the other side.

As I look back on the painful experience of my childhood, I am overwhelmed with gratitude to God for answering my early prayers. He heard the desperate cries of a ten-year-old girl who could offer Him nothing in return. I had no status, no special abilities, no money to contribute. My father was not a physician or a lawyer or a member of the city council. I was totally without dignity or social influence. Yet the Creator of the Universe entered my little room and communed with me about the difficulties I was experiencing. It was awesome to realize that He loved me just as I was, and my pain became His pain. What a magnificent God we serve!

Is there any wonder why I believe literally in the Scripture that promises, "Trust in the Lord with all thine heart and lean not unto thine own understanding. In all thy ways acknowledge Him, and He shall direct thy paths?" (Proverbs 3:5-6, KJV).

I have provided this background to explain why the topic for our book has become so important to me. My early home, by necessity, had no traditions whatsoever. At Christmas time, for example, we never knew if we would be able to afford a tree or gifts to put under it. There was no special dinner or even any forethought for the holidays. Yuletide was just another financial hurdle to be scaled.

But when I married into the Dobson family, I saw the glorious meaning of loving interdependency throughout the year. The Dobsons are a proud southern family that is steeped in tradition. Many of their annual festivals are centered around customary meals. My husband, Jim, says, "The great value of traditions comes as they give a family a sense of identity, a belongingness. All of us desperately need to feel that we're not just a cluster of people living together in a house, but we're a family that's conscious of its uniqueness, its personality, character and heritage, and that our special relationships of love and companionship make us a unit with identity and personality."

These words contain great wisdom for meaningful family life, and we are attempting to implement them in our home. In fact, the purpose for this book is to help you establish similar traditions in your home. Gloria and I have prepared a "how to" book that we hope will enrich the lives of your children and loved ones.

Today is the last day of your past and the first day of your future. There's no better time than now to begin "making memories" with your precious family.

MAKING MEMORABLE HOLIDAYS / SPECIAL DAYS

THIS DAY

There is beauty in the morning
    With the sun tip-toeing in,
When the day's a brand new conscience
    And the world's a chance to win.

There is muscle in the noontime
    When the sun is plowing through
Hot and bright and clear and brawny,
    Nature's time to go and do.

There's a charm about the evening—
    Gentle, loving like a friend,
Smiling o'er the west horizon,
    Tying up the day's loose ends.

Lovely, complicated wrappings
    Sheath the gift of one-day-more;
Breathless, I untie the package—
    Never lived _this_ day before!

Gloria Gaither

From _Rainbows Live At Easter_
Copyright © 1974 by Gloria Gaither

ON NEW YEAR'S EVE

A TIME TO REFLECT

- On New Year's Eve, give each family member an unlighted candle.

- Lower the lights and select one person to be the "candle lighter."

- As each family member's candle is lighted, have him or her make one request of God for the coming year: help in meeting a new goal, maintaining a priority, working on a better relationship with another family member, or other similar requests.

- Close with a prayer of thanksgiving for God's provision and protection during the past year.

- Serve a traditional snack—soup and a cheese tray, or other favorite combination.

CHAMP FOR THE YEAR

- On New Year's Eve, while waiting for midnight, choose a family game that all can play—Yahtzee, Sorry, Monopoly, or other favorite.

- Record the winner for the coming year in the lid of the box. Over the years it will be fun to see who reigned as the New Year's "champ" from one December 31 to the next December 31.

SPECIAL DAYS / THE NEW YEAR

HAPPY NEW YEAR

FAMILY DIARY

- Begin a "family diary" on the first day of the new year.

- Take turns writing about events and activities that occur on each day or week throughout the year.

- At the end of the year, schedule an evening to review and discuss the happenings of the previous twelve months.

CHILD'S SPECIAL WEEKEND

- At the beginning of the new year, designate *one* weekend during the coming twelve months for each child and write those dates on the master calendar.

- Let each child choose the activities he or she prefers on his or her special weekend, such as backpacking, fishing, bicycling, skating, visiting the zoo, or other practical possibility.

- When the children are grown, they should have a storehouse of special memories that were built during these family weekend experiences.

FAMILY FUN THROUGHOUT THE YEAR

MATERIALS NEEDED

Decorated coffee can
Colored construction paper
3" x 3" cardboard patterns,
   one for each family member
Scissors
Pencils

- During the first week of the New Year, place a colorfully decorated coffee can near the kitchen table. Label it "Family Fun Throughout the Year."

- Give each member of the family a different colored piece of construction paper, scissors, pencils, and a 3" x 3" cardboard pattern.

- Trace the square pattern five times on the construction paper and cut out the squares.

- Have each person write on each of their squares a family activity which he or she would like to do on "Family Fun" night. Then drop the slips of paper in the container.

- Each week, draw one activity from the can. The person whose color was selected one week does not get another turn until all the other colors have been chosen. This method gives every individual a turn to choose an activity and adds mystery and excitement to the evening.

- Replenish the coffee can with new cards when all the suggestions have been implemented.

HOMEMADE VALENTINES

Make your own valentines for family members.
The handmade ones are still the best.

- Cut an 8½ x 11 sheet of construction paper in half.

- Fold each half double (each full sheet will make two cards).

- Decorate cover with hearts, pictures, lace, doilies, ribbons, etc.

- Compose a poem or verse for your loved one, or write a short essay on "This Is What You Mean To Me" or "You're Something Special Because . . ."

- Copy inside card.

- Envelopes to fit this size card can be purchased at stationery stores or can be made by hand.

MATERIALS NEEDED

White and red construction paper
Lace, bits of ribbon or yarn, paper doilies, or other decorative materials
White glue
Crayons or markers
Old magazines

BELOVED SILHOUETTES

- Use a slide projector or Viewmaster to project the head profile silhouette of each person in the family onto a blank wall. A bright lamp with the shade removed also provides a good light source.

- Hold poster board against the wall and trace the silhouette with a broad-tipped pen or marker.

- Cut out each silhouette.

- Cut a heart shape from a sheet of red construction paper or poster board larger than the size of the silhouette.

- Paste each silhouette on a separate heart and display them along a hallway or send them to grandparents for valentines.

HINT: A heart-shaped paper doily may be pasted under the silhouette, using contrasting colors. For instance, use a red heart with a white doily placed on it. Then paste the red or black silhouette on top of doily.

MATERIALS NEEDED

Slide projector, Viewmaster,
   or other bright light source
Poster board
Red construction paper
Broad-tipped felt pen or marker
Scissors
Paper doilies (optional)

SPECIAL DAYS / VALENTINE'S DAY

VALENTINE TREASURE HUNT

- Buy a package of inexpensive children's valentines.

- Write a different love note on each of ten to fifteen cards; or write one word per card to form a message of love.

- Hide the cards throughout the house, in the car, or in other suitable places.

- Give a written clue on the outside of each envelope directing your "Valentine" to the next card.

- Include a small "love gift" with the last valentine.

VALENTINE NOTES

LOVE GIFT MESSAGES

• Write notes of "love" to *each* member of your family.

• Tell them why you love and appreciate them. Be specific!

• Tuck the notes in their lunch box, notebook, or briefcase, along with a special valentine treat.

CHINESE FORTUNE COOKIE NOTES

• Buy a bag of Chinese fortune cookies.

• Carefully pull the fortunes out from the cookies with a pair of tweezers.

• Cut up small slips of paper and write your *own* messages of love either in one sentence or on several pieces of paper that must be fitted together like a puzzle. The messages can also be made clever or funny if the occasion dictates

SPECIAL DAYS / VALENTINE'S DAY

HOW MOM AND DAD MET

- With the family gathered around, Dad and Mom tell the story of their first date and their courtship. They may include:

  How and where they met.
  Activities and places they enjoyed while dating.
  When they fell in love.
  What qualities attracted them to one another.
  How Dad proposed.
  Humorous stories about their courtship.

- Have Dad and Mom show old pictures of themselves when they were young.

- As a nice touch, Dad can show the family how he kissed Mom the very first time!

PASSOVER (BACKGROUND)

God commanded in Exodus 12 that this day be kept. Passover is the celebration of God's delivering His people out of the slavery of Pharaoh. The word "passover" comes from the night of the worst plague God sent to Egypt because Pharaoh, the Egyptian ruler, would not let the people go free. (Read about the plagues in Exodus 7-12.)

On that night, God promised that He would visit every house to execute judgment and would take the life of the first-born son unless that family had marked the door of their house with the blood of a perfect lamb. If a family obeyed God and marked their doors, He would "pass over" that house and no one in that family would die.

This plague finally convinced Pharaoh to let God's people go. Even to this day, Jewish families and many Christian families celebrate the feast of Passover, as God instructed. Jesus and His disciples were Israelites, and it was this celebration that He shared with His disciples as His last supper with them.

All Christians celebrate communion—the breaking of bread and sharing of the cup of wine—because Jesus instructed His followers to remember Him in this way.

The father or grandfather is seated at the head of the table. The dishes to be served should be where the father can pass them to the family.

As the meal progresses, the youngest son asks the father or grandfather the following question four different times: "Why is this night different from all other nights?"

The first time the son asks the question, the father answers as he serves the unleavened bread: "For on other nights we eat bread, but tonight we eat only *matzoth*." Then he explains the meaning of this bread.

The second time, the father answers: "For on other nights we eat other vegetables, but tonight we eat only bitter herbs." He serves the *maror* and then explains the reason.

The third time, the father answers the son's question this way: "For on other nights we do not dip our vegetables even once; but tonight —we dip twice." Salt-water is then passed and the father explains that it represents tears of sorrow. The parsley represents the new life, but we dip it in salt-water to remind us of the tears and the sacrifice that was made to make springtime and new life possible. Next, we dip the bitter herbs in *haroseth*, which sweetens the bitterness of the herb and reminds us that the sacrifice was sweetened by freedom. The color of the *haroseth* reminds us of the mortar the Hebrew slaves had to use to erect buildings for their masters.

A fourth time the youngest son asks the ritual question, to which his father answers: "For all other nights we eat sitting up, but tonight we all recline." Then he explains that in the old days free men sat on soft chairs or on couches, but servants had to stand before their masters or, while eating, sit on a hard bench. "Tonight, we celebrate our deliverance and freedom, so we sit in comfort and enjoy our freedom, wishing the same for all people."

This meal should end for Christians with the explanation that we are all "chosen people" if we have been "born" into God's family by believing in His Son, Jesus, as our Messiah. As God's people, then, we should share the cup of joy with others out of gratitude that Jesus became the final "Lamb" to be sacrificed in order that "our joy may be full."

SPECIAL DAYS / PASSOVER

SPECIAL DAYS / PASSOVER

THE PASSOVER SEDER (SUPPER)

Passover lasts seven or eight days and begins with a meal and worship service Jewish families call Seder, or "order" because they always keep the celebration in a certain order. This first meal is made up of certain foods. Each has a special meaning.

To celebrate Seder you would serve:

- *Matzoth*—wafers of unleavened bread. (Can be secured from a Jewish delicatessen or from some grocers.) This is to remind us of the fact that the Israelites did not have time to wait for yeast bread to rise because they had to be ready to move when God said. For Christians, this reminds us also to live so that we are always "ready to go" when Jesus returns. Also, yeast sometimes represented the evil in the world. God wants His people to be pure.

- *Maror*—bitter herbs, usually freshly grated horse-radish or other bitter, pungent vegetable such as onion. These herbs are a reminder of the bitter suffering in Egyptian slavery. This also reminds us that many have suffered that we may know the joy of the good news of Jesus. So in our celebration, we remember the great cost.

- *Haroseth*—a mixture of chopped apples, nuts, cinnamon, and wine. This represents the mortar with which the Israelites were forced to make bricks to build Pharaoh's great cities. (See Exodus 2:11–14 and 5:4–23.)

- *The shank bone of a lamb.* This is a symbol of the lamb that was sacrificed for sins. To Christians, this represents Jesus, God's own gift of a perfect Lamb for the sins of all.

- *A roasted egg*—an egg hard boiled in the shell. Symbol of the free-will offering that was given with the lamb. This represents giving more to God than just what is demanded. This is a gift of love. Jesus was God's ultimate gift. God's law demanded only justice, but with the gift of Jesus, God gave us more than justice; He gave us mercy, love and forgiveness.

- *Parsley or watercress.* These two plants stay green the year around and represent the continual rebirth of growing things. To Christians, this represents God's gift of everlasting life because of the resurrection.

- *Wine or grape juice.* Wine represents joy. As the service proceeds, as each plague is mentioned, each person sips a little of the wine. This means that until total liberation, joy was incomplete. Jesus said at the Last Supper that the wine represented His own life's blood, poured out for us. He meant that He must die so that we could know the total joy of freedom and forgiveness.

- *Elijah's cup.* In the center of the table is placed a goblet of wine that represents Elijah, whom the Israelites believed would foretell the coming of the Messiah. This cup remains full to welcome Elijah and his announcement of the Messiah's return. Christians believe that John the Baptist was this "Elijah." Jesus said in Matthew 11:14 that if the people could understand what was happening, they would recognize John as the promised Elijah who was to announce the Messiah's coming. For Christians, this cup does not remain untouched, but is shared by everyone at the table in the joy that our hope has come true. The Messiah has come to us and is alive to give our lives eternal joy.

SPECIAL DAYS / PASSOVER

SYMBOLS OF EASTER

Many times we enjoy the symbols of a special day without really understanding their meaning. Easter symbols are especially rich in meaning. Before Easter we might discuss the meanings of these symbols we so enjoy.

- *Spring.* Easter and spring belong together. What a wonderful time to celebrate newness of life and the resurrection when all nature is "rising again."

- *Baby bunnies, chicks, birds.* All newly born creatures remind us of the new birth in Christ. Because of Easter we can become "new creatures" in Him.

- The *green, yellow, pink,* and *lavender* colors of springtime. These are perfect to symbolize Easter. Earth bursts forth into color with the proclamation "Life wins!" Green also stands for new life, and lavender, the color of royalty, reminds us that Jesus is King of Kings and Lord of Lords.

- *New clothes.* A new outfit symbolizes the putting away of winter—the time when it seems all nature hides "in the tomb"—and the dressing up of the earth in the lovely new clothes of summer. We, too, because of Christ's bursting from the tomb, are "clothed in newness of life."

- *Eggs.* Eggs, of course, are the epitome of promised life—life sealed away for a time before new life literally bursts forth! Eggs also symbolize in Jewish tradition a free-will offering, the giving of more than is demanded. Jesus is God's free-will offering. God gives us far beyond what we deserve or even dare to ask. Jesus is the gift not only of life, but of eternal life!

"JESUS IS RISEN"

Children *love* to decorate hard-boiled eggs.

• Try writing messages on the eggs with crayons before dyeing to remind us of the real meaning of Easter. Examples of messages are:

"Jesus Loves You"

"Love—Forever"

"Jesus Died For You"

"Born Again"

"He Is Risen"

"Love Changes Things"

"Hallelujah"

EASTER MOSAICS

MATERIALS NEEDED

Large sheet of poster board
Old crayons, assorted colors
Glue

- Trace or draw a simple Easter picture onto a piece of poster board.

- Remove all paper from old crayons.

- Cut crayons into pieces ¼- to ½-inch long.

- Stand crayon pieces on end and glue them to picture, filling areas in solid with colors to match those used in picture.

- Display your crayon mosaic.

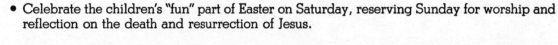

EASTER SATURDAY

- Celebrate the children's "fun" part of Easter on Saturday, reserving Sunday for worship and reflection on the death and resurrection of Jesus.

- Hide eggs and Easter baskets on Saturday, including a special "treasure egg."

- Buy or make a large plastic or papier-maché egg. Enclose a small "treasure" inside the egg such as money, a gift, a candy treat, or a small toy.

- Hide the special egg carefully. It is best for the children to find the other eggs before locating the "treasure egg." This increases the suspense and competition as children search for the "hidden treasure."

- Decorate your table with an Easter theme, and serve refreshments after the hunt.

SPECIAL DAYS / EASTER

FAMILY EASTER EGG HUNT

- Collect the plastic eggs in which L'eggs hose are sold, or buy plastic eggs. Real eggs may be hard-boiled and colored if desired.

- Put one small prize in each plastic egg.

- Hide all eggs ahead of time.

- Talk about why eggs can be symbols of Easter, for example, to represent the promise of new life that the tomb held for us all.

- Give each person (grown-ups, too) a paper lunch sack decorated with an Easter sticker.

- Begin the hunt with a starting signal.

- After about ten to fifteen minutes, blow a whistle, calling everyone in.

- Take turns showing each other the treasures found.

- Pass out prizes to everyone, or celebrate with Easter cake and milk or other beverage.

FAMILY COMMUNION

AHEAD OF TIME

• Read about Passover and what it meant from a Bible story book or from the Bible (see Exodus 12).

• Explain why the Jewish families ate unleavened bread when they remembered Passover.

• Read passages leading up to the account of the Last Supper (John 13), Jesus' last words to His disciples (John 14–16), and Jesus' prayer for us (John 17).

• Explain that Jesus became the Passover Lamb as a sacrifice for our sins forever.

• Discuss what it means to share His cup (John 18:11).

• Discuss what it means to be part of the Body of Christ.

• Be sure the children understand and participate with reverence.

SHARING THE ELEMENTS OF THE FAMILY COMMUNION

• Use one loaf of unleavened bread and one cup so that the family may share "One Body" and "One Cup." (If it is your conviction that only a clergyman must administer communion, invite your clergyman to do so in the circle of your family.)

• It is meaningful to share with each person with whom you break bread why you feel that person has been a gift from God to you. Jesus said "I love you" with a cross. We need to practice freely saying it to each other.

• Thank God together for the gift of His Son, for forgiveness, and for adopting each of us into His own family, making us sons and daughters of God and brothers and sisters with the Lord Jesus, who brought us to the Father with His own Life.

SPECIAL DAYS / EASTER

FAMILY SUNRISE SERVICE

AHEAD OF TIME

- Choose a special, quiet place from which the sunrise can be seen.

- Prepare a simple, carry-along breakfast of boiled eggs, rolls, juice, etc. (If you like, each person's breakfast could be packed in a colorful Easter basket. Surprises could be hidden in the bottom of each basket.

- Find and mark the Easter story in the Bible.

- Choose one or two songs the whole family can sing about the risen Lord, or take along a cassette player and taped music the family can sing along with.

- The week before Easter, read from a Bible story book or from the Bible the events leading up to the Resurrection (Matthew 26, 27) and discuss them.

- The night before Easter, talk about how the disciples must have felt on the Saturday night before the Resurrection; how Jesus' mother must have felt; what Mary Magdalene and those who had known Jesus were feeling.

EASTER MORNING

- Rise early enough to give the family time to get to your special place just before the sun comes up.

- Wear clothes that can be gotten into quickly (you can get ready for church later). Take warm jackets and blankets.

- Spread a blanket to sit on; then read together about the women going to Jesus' tomb and what they experienced.

- As the sun comes peeping over the horizon, sing or play a victorious song. Then thank God *with your eyes wide open* for the Resurrection and what it means to your family.

- Celebrate by sharing the simple breakfast you have brought with you.

TRADITIONAL EASTER BRUNCH

Plan your own traditional brunch. Serve the same foods each year. A sample menu might include: orange juice, fresh fruit, scrambled eggs, crisp bacon, and apple muffins.

The recipe provided here is a Dobson favorite. It was given to Shirley by a dear friend whose mother made apple muffins every Saturday morning.

EASTER APPLE MUFFINS

   1 cup chopped apples
     (apples should be pared and
     thinly sliced, ¼-in., before
     chopping)
   ¼ cup sugar
   1 egg (well-beaten)
   ⅔ cup milk
   ¼ cup butter

   •

   2 cups flour
   ½ tsp. salt
   ½ tsp. cinnamon
   ¼ cup sugar
   4 tsp. baking powder

TOPPING:

   4 tbsp. melted butter
   2 tbsp. sugar
   1 tsp. cinnamon

In large bowl mix together apples and ¼ cup sugar. Blend in egg. Add milk and butter and mix together lightly. Sift in dry ingredients: flour, salt, cinnamon, sugar, and baking powder. Mix together well. Spoon into greased or paper-lined muffin tins. In separate bowl mix together topping. Add topping to each muffin. Bake at 350 degrees for 20 minutes. Serves 12.

SPECIAL DAYS / PATRIOTIC DAYS

JULY 4 PATRIOT PARADE

AHEAD OF TIME

• Send or call invitations to family and friends to join in the parade.

• Decorate everything that has wheels (bikes, trikes, wagons, "Big Wheels," doll buggies) with red, white, or blue paper stars, crepe-paper streamers, ribbons, etc.

• Have each person who is going to be in the parade choose a patriot to represent. Collect or make suitable costumes from crepe paper, construction paper, and grown-ups' old clothes. Some possible characters: George Washington, Betsy Ross, Uncle Sam, Abraham Lincoln, Daniel Boone, Davy Crockett, Paul Revere, Martha Washington, a bugler, a drummer.

• Get the family pets into the act by tying bright red, white, or blue ribbons, bows, or strips of paper to leashes, collars, cages, or pet boxes—even fishbowls.

NOTE: Be careful not to put pets close together who don't like each other (or who like each other too well).

AT THE SCHEDULED TIME

• Have those not in the parade sit in lawn chairs where they can see the "parade route."

• Announce the beginning of the parade with a bugle call, after which the drummer(s) lead off the procession.

• Have the announcer introduce each patriot or parade entry as that "act" goes by the stands.

• After the parade, have the announcer invite everyone to join in singing "America the Beautiful."

• Serve everyone juicy cold slices of watermelon.

• With adult supervision, sparklers or other fireworks can be added as a finale.

UNSCRAMBLE THE CODE*

- Select an appropriate Bible verse; for example, 2 Chronicles 7:14.

- Write it on a piece of paper in the following code form:

  IEFEMEYEPEEEOEPELEEEWEHEIECE
  HEAEREEECEAELELEEEDEBEYEMEYE
  NEAEMEEESEHEAELELE . . . etc.

- Give the family several minutes to decipher the code.

- If the code is still unsolved after ten minutes, give clues as necessary, waiting two or three minutes after each clue before giving the next one. Such clues could be:

  1. The letter "E" separates the letters and the words.
  2. Look up 2 Chronicles 7:14.

- Have each family member write down the words. When everyone has finished, quote the verse together.

- Allow some time to memorize the verse. See who can memorize it first

- Discuss how the Scripture applies to America. Ask relevant questions: Is God forgotten in our country? How? Is He honored? How?

* Appreciation is expressed to *Family Life Today* for use of this idea.

PATRIOTIC GIFTS

A PRESENT FOR OUR LAND

- Plan to give a living and growing present to our land. Planting a tree or bush would be a great family project.

- Discuss what kind of plant should be selected and where it would grow best.

- Talk about the positive reasons for giving such a gift: it releases oxygen into the atmosphere; it gives shelter to the birds; it provides beauty and shade, etc.

- Plant the tree or bush in your own yard, or ask the city or park services to select an appropriate spot for it in the community.

- Plan how to care for your plant.

JULY 4 "WE LOVE YOU AMERICA" DINNER

- Plan an all-American dinner including such traditional foods as hot dogs, hamburgers, apple pie, ice cream, etc.

- Decorate the table with a patriotic theme, using red, white, and blue napkins, tablecloth, flowers, etc.

- If a globe is available, point out the United States to the young children. Talk about the countries which surround it, the customs of the people, and reasons people love the countries they live in.

- Look in the encyclopedia for the article discussing this special holiday and read it aloud.

- Discuss the article as a family. Ask each child to recite one important fact or idea he or she learned.

- This dinner can be served on other patriotic days besides July 4: Memorial Day, Flag Day, Veterans' Day, Washington's or Lincoln's birthdays, etc.

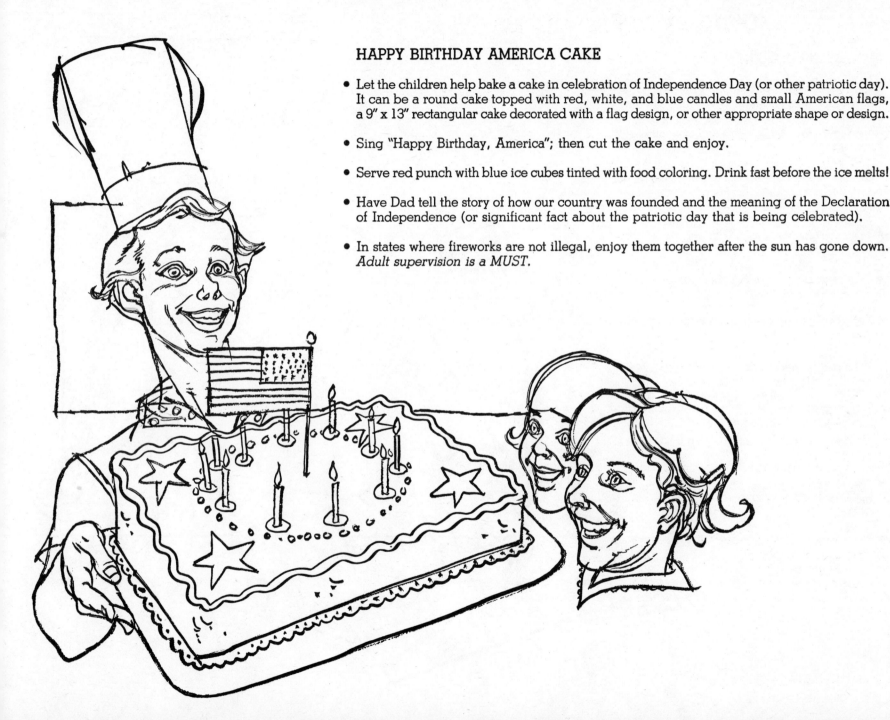

HAPPY BIRTHDAY AMERICA CAKE

- Let the children help bake a cake in celebration of Independence Day (or other patriotic day). It can be a round cake topped with red, white, and blue candles and small American flags, a 9" x 13" rectangular cake decorated with a flag design, or other appropriate shape or design.

- Sing "Happy Birthday, America"; then cut the cake and enjoy.

- Serve red punch with blue ice cubes tinted with food coloring. Drink fast before the ice melts!

- Have Dad tell the story of how our country was founded and the meaning of the Declaration of Independence (or significant fact about the patriotic day that is being celebrated).

- In states where fireworks are not illegal, enjoy them together after the sun has gone down. *Adult supervision is a MUST.*

WORK

GOD'S PERFECT PLAN

Work was always a part of God's plan. The first thing God gave to Adam was a job: to name all living things, and "to dress" and "to keep" the garden. Work was a gift and was intended to be a joy.

Make banners to put up in your house to celebrate God's plan for work. Here are some suggestions:

- "The firmament showeth His handiwork." (Ps. 19:16)

- "We must do the work of Him who sent Me." (John 9:4, NIV)

- "We are workers together with God." (1 Cor. 3:9)

- "The people had a mind to work." (Neh. 4:6)

- "Be strong . . . and work, for I am with you." (Hag. 2:4)

- "He is the Rock, His work is perfect." (Deut. 32:4)

- "Be a workman who does not need to be ashamed." (2 Tim. 2:15)

THE GIFT OF WORK

To help your children appreciate the gift of work, make arrangements ahead of time to take them to your place of employment on a regular work day, or if that is impossible, collect materials, pictures, or artifacts that will demonstrate the work you do.

• Begin the day by talking about the gift that work is to our lives and the joy we find in contributing to other persons' lives through our skills.

• Take an outing to your place of employment. (If both parents work, include both places of employment.)

• Show the facility, your special place of work, and introduce the children to some of the persons with whom you work.

• Let the children learn about the end result of your specific job. You may want to eat together in the plant cafeteria, office snack shop, or nearby restaurant where you often go for lunch. If you take your lunch, pack a lunch for each person in the family and eat together at your usual place.

• At the end of the day, discuss the jobs each person in the family does to make the home run smoothly. Thank God for the health, strength, and intelligence to work.

GREAT QUOTES

A lot has been said about work. Make a collection of great quotes about work and type or print the ones you like the best on strips of colored paper. Tack them in random design on a family bulletin board or tape them to doors about the house. See the illustration for suggestions.

At supper on Labor Day, require as admission fee to the supper table, the recitation of one memorized quote about work.

MY FAMILY'S WORK HERITAGE

Make a game of a family research project. See who can find out the most about what your ancestors did for their life's work.

- Buy each family member a spiral notebook for keeping notes and compiling "work profiles."

- Use a cassette recorder to "document" bits of interesting information.

POSSIBLE SOURCES OF INFORMATION

- Interview older family members and ask information about the types of work skills of members of your family tree.

- Find your family's genealogy (most families have one member who is interested in completing this document) and read to find interesting occupations. Old family Bibles often give information about what family members did for a living.

- Make a list of the most famous and infamous "workers" in your family's history.

- Make a list of times in history when the need for work changed the course of family history.

- Make a list of what the young people in your family think they might like to do as their life's work.

- List vocations that are available today that did not exist two generations ago.

- Thank God for the wide opportunity for work available to us today. Thank Him for each person's specialness and the chance to express that uniqueness in the work we do.

SPECIAL DAYS / LABOR DAY

HALLOWEEN PUMPKIN HUNT

AHEAD OF TIME

Find out about places in your area where pumpkins are grown and make arrangements to visit one with your family about a week before Halloween. If there is no such place, begin in early spring to grow your own pumpkins. Consult a gardener for instructions for your locale that will produce some fine pumpkins by Halloween.

- Make a family outing of the pumpkin-finding hunt, allowing each person (parents, too) to choose one pumpkin.

- If apple cider is available at the pumpkin farm, have a glass of it together, or take a gallon of cider home to enjoy later.

- When you arrive home, if the weather permits, spread several layers of newspaper on the driveway before beginning work on the pumpkins. (You may have to work inside the house or i.. the garage.)

- Carve or draw faces on the pumpkins, each person creating his/her own masterpiece. If there are young children, Magic Markers should be used instead of knives.

- If pumpkins are carved (save some seeds to roast), put a candle inside each jack-o-lantern (a little melted wax will keep candle upright).

- Display jack-o-lanterns in a row.

- After supper, as it gets dark, make some hot spiced cider and pop some corn. (See recipe for hot cider on page 110.)

- Have one grown-up or older child light jack-o-lanterns. Then go out together to see the spooky results.

- Serve everyone some hot cider and popcorn.

RECIPE FOR ROASTED PUMPKIN SEEDS

- Obtain a fresh pumpkin.

- Cut into the pumpkin and separate seeds from pulp.

- Wash seeds in a colander.

- Drain them on several layers of paper towel.

- In a large skillet, melt 2 tbsp. margarine (butter scorches more easily). Add 1 tsp. salt.

- Add 2 cups pumpkin seeds and sauté about 3 minutes, stirring so that all seeds are coated with margarine.

- Place seeds on a cookie sheet and bake for about 25 minutes in an oven preheated to 300 degrees.

- Drain on a paper towel until pumpkin seeds are crisp and cool enough to eat.

HALLOWEEN FUN

THE NIGHT BEFORE HALLOWEEN

- Carve out a pumpkin and place a candle and small amount of dry ice inside. The ice will release a spooky vapor. An adult should handle these to avoid the danger of burns from the ice or candle.

- Set an eerie atmosphere with decorations and lighting effects.

- Let the children dress up in their costumes and masks. Discuss the characters they are pretending to be.

- Talk about the different kinds of invisible masks we sometimes wear. Why do we wear them?

- Let each member of the family share some of their fears—real or imaginary. Discuss how these might be diminished or dispelled.

- For refreshments, serve Halloween cupcakes and orange soda.

SPECIAL DAYS / HALLOWEEN

DESIGN-YOUR-OWN HALLOWEEN COSTUME

• Obtain a piece of wrapping paper equal in length to your child's height.

• A week before Halloween, have your small child lie down on the piece of wrapping paper, and trace around him with a broad-tipped pen or marker.

• Cut out the shape you have traced.

• Let the child draw directly onto the shape with crayons the design of the Halloween costume he would like.

• Mom will then try to make a costume according to the design the child has created.

THANKSGIVING AT THE DOBSONS . . .

Thanksgiving is given major prominence in the Dobson home. It marks the beginning of the holiday season and the happy gathering with relatives who live close by. When the day arrives, excitement and anticipation fill the air. Wonderful mouth-watering aromas of turkey, dressing, and applie pies float from the kitchen as family members arrive. A new jigsaw puzzle is placed on the card table with a pot of hot coffee nearby. Various lawn games are set up in the backyard and a spirited basketball game is soon organized on the driveway.

When dinnertime is announced, we gather around the table and Jim reads a Scripture. Everyone takes the hand of the person sitting next to him and Jim prays a prayer of thankfulness to God. After the traditional meal has been eaten and the table is cleared for dessert, two kernels of dried Indian corn are placed beside each plate. I explain that this represents the first Thanksgiving when the Pilgrims came to America and endured such a difficult winter and how grateful they were to God for bringing them through. A little basket is then passed around and as each kernel is dropped into the basket, we describe two blessings for which we are most thankful. The comments invariably focus on loved ones, expressed with deepest feelings and appreciation. By the time the basket returns to where it started, people are usually crying. It happens every year. It's a time of affirmation when we share our need for one another, and thank God for the family He has given us. This experience becomes more meaningful each year because of the inexorable march of time and its effect on the older generations among us. We have been painfully aware in recent years that two special people are now absent from the family circle, Jim's father and my uncle. But we are grateful for each member of our small family who has survived another year.

I am reminded at this moment of a prayer expressed by Jim's father during the final year of his life. We had been to Kansas City for a visit and were on the way to the airport at the end of that pleasant vacation. Jim asked his dad to say a prayer before we were separated. I'll never forget his words, spoken in the car as we approached the airport.

He said, "Lord, we have enjoyed being together so much this past week, and you have been good to make this time possible. But Lord, we are realistic enough to know that life moves on, and that circumstances will not always be as we enjoy them today. We understand that a day is coming when the fellowship we now share will be but a memory to those who remain. That's why I want to thank you for bringing love into our lives for this season, and for the happiness we have experienced with one another."

Two weeks later, my father-in-law suffered a massive heart attack from which he never recovered. And his final prayer is his legacy to us, today. Circumstances will inevitably change; nothing in this life is eternal or permanent. But while God grants us breath, we will enjoy one another to the fullest and spread our love as far and wide as possible.

Thanksgiving at the Dobson home is an occasion for the celebration of that philosophy.

SPECIAL DAYS / THANKSGIVING

THANKSGIVING HOSPITALITY

- As a loving tradition, invite a few guests to dinner who have no family and nowhere to go on Thanksgiving Day.

- A few days before Thanksgiving, ask each guest to recall two or three of his or her favorite dishes.

- Serve one of each guest's favorite dishes with your turkey dinner. Your guests will be *delightfully* thankful for your hospitality.

CREATE A "CENTERPIECE"

As a family project, create your own traditional centerpiece to be used each year on your Thanksgiving table. It can be as simple or as complex as you choose. Be creative! The family will enjoy seeing the arrangement year after year.

SUGGESTIONS

Pilgrim salt and pepper shakers
Papier-mâché turkey
Paper-folded turkey
Horn of plenty filled with fresh fruits, vegetables, and nuts
Dried flower arrangement

"THANK YOU" PLACE CARDS

- Fold unlined 3 x 5 cards in half to make place cards for every person at the Thanksgiving table.

- Decorate the cards in a Thanksgiving theme.

- Write each person's name on the front of a card.

- On the inside, write a personal thank-you message. Make each message personal, truthful, and specific, for example: "You always remember my birthday," "Thank you for being such a thoughtful aunt," etc.

NOTE: Larger cards can be used if desired so that each member of the family can write a message to every other person having dinner—all on the same card. Each individual then receives more than one expression of gratitude and from more than one person. It's fun to know just what makes others appreciate you.

"I'M THANKFUL FOR . . ."

- Play the game "Twenty Questions," basing it on things for which each person is thankful, such as a favorite food, home, pet, country, etc.

- The person who is "it" thinks of one thing for which he or she is thankful, and the others try to guess what it is by asking him questions which he can answer "yes" or "no."

- If the group cannot guess the answer in twenty questions or less, the person who is "it" is the winner.

SPECIAL DAYS / THANKSGIVING

THANKS FOR WILDLIFE TREE

On Thanksgiving, after dinner is finished, christen the Christmas season by decorating the first tree—an outdoor Christmas gift for the wildlife in your neighborhood. Make any or all of the following suggestions and use them to trim the tree. There will be many hours of delightful bird- and squirrel-watching as you share these gifts with God's creatures.

SUGGESTED MATERIALS

    ground suet
    stale bread crumbs
    bird seed
    emptied orange or grapefruit halves
    pipe cleaners
    pine cones
    peanut butter
    cranberries
    popped corn
    raisins
    15" pieces of floral wire
    peanuts (unshelled and unsalted)
    heavy thread
    stale doughnuts

- Protect your working area with newspaper or plastic before assembling the gifts described below.

- Mix ground suet with seeds or stale bread crumbs and fill empty orange or grapefruit halves with the mixture. Attach pipe cleaner at three places around the edge; join them at center and twist to form a hook to hang feeder on branches.

- Spread pine cones with peanut butter and roll them in bird seed. Attach a pipe cleaner for a hanger.

- String cranberries, popcorn, and raisins on pieces of floral wire. Bend wire and attach ends to form a circle that can be hung over the ends of the branches.

- Tie peanuts along a piece of heavy thread and tie onto tree.

- Tie stale doughnuts to tree with thread or floral wire.

MELTED CRAYON ART

- From the old crayons that may have accumulated among your children's toys, gather up a good selection in fall colors.

- Use a crayon sharpener or vegetable peeler to turn the crayons into shavings. Keep colors separate in small Dixie cups or baby food jars.

- On art paper or manila paper, draw an outline of a Thanksgiving object such as a turkey, pumpkin, horn of plenty, fall leaf, etc.

- Place drawing on ironing board, first protecting ironing board cover with a layer of waxed paper. Lightly sprinkle shavings to color in areas of picture.

- Carefully cover picture with waxed paper.

- Iron carefully, heating iron on low, and apply pressure just long enough to melt shavings onto paper.

- Allow drawing to cool slightly.

- Remove waxed paper and hang your work of art You may want to cut out your drawing before hanging.

MEMORIES OF A SPECIAL CHRISTMAS

If everything special and warm and happy in my formative years could have been consolidated into one word, that word would have been *Christmas*. So, by the time the building blocks of my days had piled themselves into something as formidable as late adolescence, Christmas had a lot to live up to.

Christmas, by then, meant fireplaces and the bustle of a big excited family, complete with aunts, uncles, and cousins. It meant great smells from the kitchen—homemade bread and cranberries bubbling on the stove, pumpkin pies and turkey. It meant Grandma's cheery voice racing to be the first to holler "Christmas Gift!" as we came in the door. It meant real cedar Christmas trees, handmade foil ornaments, and lots of secrets. It meant enfolding in the arms of our great family the lonely or forsaken of our village who had no place to go. It meant all the good and lovely things we said about Christmas being in the heart and the joy being in the giving.

Then came that other year.

There were many things that conspired, as it were, to bring me to the laboratory situation in which I would test all my so glibly accepted theories. Grandma was gone, leaving in my heart a vacuum that wouldn't go away. My sister was married now and had the responsibility of sharing her holidays with her husband's people. The other relatives were far away. After a lifetime of serving in the ministry, Daddy had that year felt directed to resign his flock with no other pastures in mind and "wait on the Lord." Since I was away at college, just beginning my first year, I wasn't there when my parents moved from the parsonage to the tiny cottage at the lake which a concerned businessman had helped them build. Nor was I prepared that winter day for the deserted barrenness that can be found in resort areas built only for summertime fun.

There was no fireplace. There was no bustle of a big excited family. Gone was the sense of tradition and history that is the art of the aged to provide, and gone was the thrill of the immediate future that comes with the breathless anticipation of children.

The dinner was going to be small, for just the three of us, and there just wasn't any *ring* in the brave attempt at shouting "Christmas Gift!"

that Mother made as I came in the door. Daddy suggested that because I'd always loved it, he and I should go to the woods to cut our own tree. I knew that now, of all times, I could not let my disappointment show. I put on my boots and my cheeriest face, and off through the knee-deep snow we trudged into the Michigan woods. My heart was heavy, and I knew Mother was back at the stove fighting back the tears for all that was not there.

There was loveliness as the forest lay blanketed in its heavy comforter of snow, but there was no comforter to wrap around the chill in my heart. Daddy whistled as he chopped the small cedar tree. (He always whistled when there was something bothering him.) As the simple tuneless melody cut through the silent frozen air, I got a hint of the silent burdens adults carry, and for the first time felt myself on the brink of becoming one. So as I picked up my end of the scraggly, disappointingly small cedar, I also picked up my end of grownup responsibility. I felt the times shift. I was no longer a child to be sheltered and cared for and entertained. My folks had put good stuff in me. Now as I trudged back through the snow, watching the back of my father's head, the weary curve of his shoulders, his breath making smoke signals in the morning air, I vowed to put some good stuff back into their lives.

The day was somehow different after that. We sat around our little table stringing cranberries and making foil cut-outs. But this time it was not the activity of a child, but sort of a ceremonial tribute to the child I somehow could never again afford to be, and to the people who had filled that childhood with such wealth and beauty.

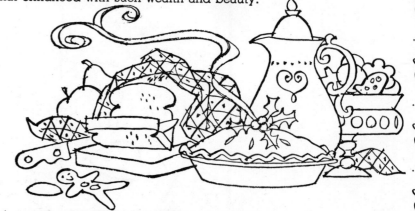

CHRISTMAS TRADITIONS TO TRY

- Start a tree-decorating tradition. Serve the *same menu* each year as you trim the tree. The children will look forward to it. (Menu suggestions: clam chowder and bread sticks; Christmas cookies and hot chocolate; Christmas cake and hot cider.)

- Each Christmas, let each of your children choose his or her *own* tree ornament. When they are grown, their ornaments will have special memories as they trim their own "family tree."

- Each Christmas, start a tradition of viewing all the family photographs, slides, and movies. It's fun to see how everyone has changed, and it stirs warm memories to reminisce about when the pictures were taken.

- On December 1, set up a card table with an appropriate jigsaw puzzle (500–1000 pieces). As guests drop in throughout the holidays, they will enjoy working on the project. The object is to complete the puzzle by Christmas.

- Set a date with another family to go caroling in the neighborhood. Close the evening with refreshments.

- Parents give elementary age children $5.00 each to buy Christmas presents for *everyone*. (You may need to adjust for inflation.)

- Honor Jesus with a special birthday party (see next page).

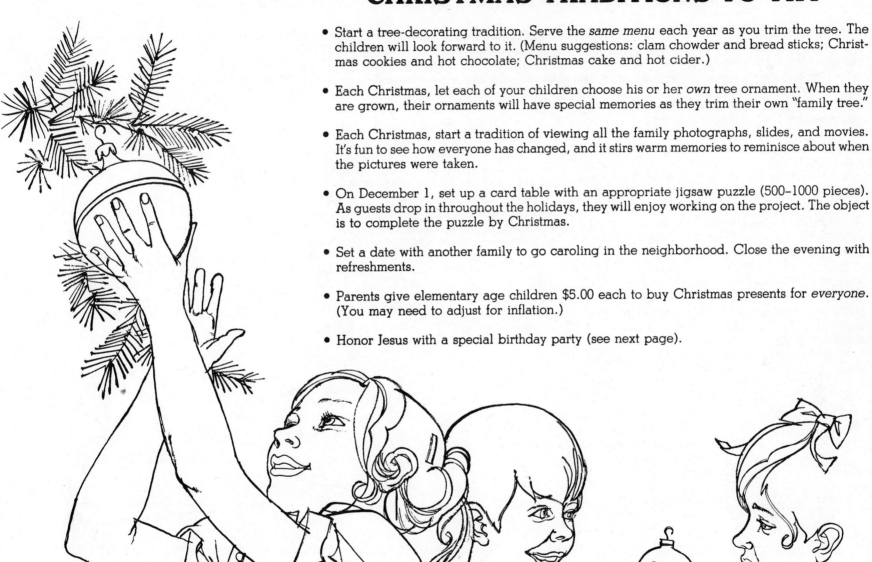

JESUS' BIRTHDAY PARTY

Have a party in honor of Him whose birth we celebrate. Include in the celebration an older person who would otherwise be alone, someone you have just met, a young person away from home, and one or two very special friends such as a pastor or teacher who is important to your family's life.

Some special things to make or do might include:

• Birthday-card place cards.

• A special star-shaped cake with white and yellow icing full of fruit, to represent the fulfillment of the seed of promise.

• A table centerpiece of a basket or small wooden box of clean straw surrounded by small packages made to represent gold, frankincense and myrrh. Someone might tell about the three gifts and what they might have represented or how they might have been used.

EXAMPLE: Gold was the most precious metal symbol of God's most precious gift. Perhaps this provided the financial means for the trip Mary, Joseph, and Jesus made to Egypt and for their stay there when they were forced to hide from Herod.

Frankincense and myrrh were important spices used in Jewish rituals as incense and as burial spices. Perhaps these gifts hinted at the fulfillment of the old Law as well as the crucifixion of Jesus that was to come. Someone has suggested that Mary may have kept these precious spices and used them to embalm the body of our Lord thirty-three years after his birth.

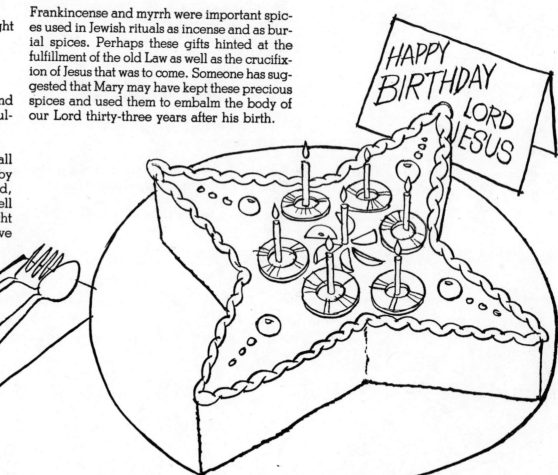

CHRISTMAS CARD ACTIVITIES

CHRISTMAS CARD DEVOTIONS

Cards can be used as a meaningful part of family devotions during the Advent season.

- Each day (or on selected days) use the cards received on that particular day, or have someone pull a specific number of cards from a basket used for this purpose.

- During family devotions, or after singing or Bible study, read the cards aloud.

- Have prayer for the families who sent the cards.

- Hang the cards up for display on the mantel, around a doorway or archway, on the back of a door, or on the Christmas tree.

CHRISTMAS CARD PRAYER LINK

Use Christmas cards as a link to real people and their needs through the Christmas season and the month of January.

- Choose one Christmas card each day from those received. Read the whole card aloud and pass it around the family circle. (Do this at a regular time like bedtime or after supper each night or at breakfast time.)

- Have special prayer together for each person in the family that sent the card.

- Send a postcard to that family to tell them about your Christmas-card prayers and that their card was the one chosen on this day. They will appreciate knowing that your family prayed today for their family.

AFTER-CHRISTMAS CARDS

- As Christmas cards come, place them in an attractive container. After Christmas is over and the household is more settled, place the container near the dinner table.

- After dinner, pass the container and let each member of the family choose one card.

- Take turns reading the cards and enjoying their beauty.

- Discuss the family or person who sent the card. Are there any specific problems or needs?

- Close your dinner hour by praying for the families or persons who sent the cards.

SPECIAL DAYS / CHRISTMAS

SPECIAL DAYS / CHRISTMAS

HOMEMADE CHRISTMAS DECORATIONS

GARLANDS FOR THE HOUSE

Make these garlands on evenings before Christmas to use on your Christmas tree or in your hallway, doorways, or stairway:

- Lifesaver garland

  1. Cut two equal strands of desired length of colorful yarn.
  2. String Lifesavers loosely on the first strand.
  3. Lay the string of candy on a table, making the Lifesavers lie flat, in one direction, end to end.
  4. With the other strand of yarn weave in and out in the opposite direction so that each candy is forced to lie flat.
  5. Secure ends of each yarn to last candy on each end.

- String Cheerios or other circular cereal pieces in the same way, using brightly colored yarn or ribbon. Be prepared to replace the garlands as they are nibbled away.

- String raw cranberries and popcorn alternately onto a piece of yarn.

- String colored marshmallows randomly or in a predetermined pattern of colors.

- Make a garland of white styrofoam packing squiggles. Watch that children do not put these in their mouths. Styrofoam is *not* edible.

- String uncooked elbow macaroni and other pasta, painting it if desired.

  HINT: Dip the end of the string or yarn in melted paraffin to make a "needle" which will be stiff and yet bend.

TREE AND PACKAGE ORNAMENTS

Take a special evening to create these ornaments to use as tree or package decorations.

- Cut shapes from cardboard and cover with foil or glitter.

- Hang sour gumdrop type fruit slices with ornament hooks that have been inserted in the top of the candy.

- Hang white-chocolate-covered pretzels.

- Wrap popcorn balls in foil or colored cellophane. Secure the wrapping with bright yarn, leaving the ends long enough for tying the balls onto the tree.

- Make cornstarch clay ornaments from recipe on page 85.

  1. While dough is warm, divide it into two portions. Use food coloring to color one red, the other green.
  2. Roll dough on waxed paper and cut into Christmas shapes with a cookie cutters.
  3. Poke a large nail through the top of each ornament to make a hole for hanging.
  4. Dry thoroughly, turning ornaments occasionally.
  5. If desired, glue glitter to parts of ornaments.

DECK THE HALLS

- Cover a large styrofoam ball with sprigs of mistletoe and hang it in an archway or doorway as an excuse for family hugs and kisses. As the mistletoe dries, take care to pick up any berries that may fall, as these are poisonous and may be ingested by small children.

- Have the family make a special time of arranging the nativity set.

- Tie ripple ribbon on ends of cellophane-wrapped mints, then tie onto styrofoam wreath.

- Make homemade taffy (see recipe, p. 114). Wrap in waxed paper bits and twist ends. Tie on tree or styrofoam wreath with yarn or string.

- Make large letters out of newspaper or construction paper spelling out "HAPPY BIRTHDAY, JESUS." Tape to large front window.

- Have each member of the family whittle from balsa wood a "Christ-mon" (Christ-monogram) to hang on the tree, such as a fish, cross, manger, star, lamb, etc. Talk about the meanings of the chosen symbol.

MAGAZINE CHRISTMAS ART

- From old magazines, tear pictures or ads that are mostly green.

- Cut the ads or pictures into pairs of strips of varying measured lengths, for example, 8 inches, 7 inches, 6 inches, 5 inches, etc.

- Turn a rectangular piece of poster board or construction paper so that the shorter sides are the top and bottom. Draw a vertical line from top to bottom midway between the left and right sides. Starting at the bottom with the longest strips of paper, glue one end of strips of equal length to each side of the vertical line (see diagram). As you add successive layers of shorter and shorter strips, slightly overlap the strips to avoid having the poster board or construction paper show through.

NOTE: This idea can be adapted to make a special Christmas card.

GROWING COLLECTION

As a part of the Christmas celebration every year, give each child an ornament of his own. When the children grow up and move into their own homes, they will have their own ornaments to take with them. These ornaments might be different for each child each year:

• crystal

• straw

• wood

• metal

• fancy designer ornament

• handmade

This collection is more than Christmas ornaments. Rather it is a collection of special memories, touched and treasured through the years.

SPECIAL DAYS / CHRISTMAS

CHRISTMAS . . . DOBSON STYLE

The Christmas season is greeted in the Dobson home with the same excitement that the approach of Thanksgiving brings. This wonderful occasion begins with decorating the house during the first week in December. Hanging on either side of the fireplace are large red "stockings" that bear the names of our children. Early each Christmas morning, these are filled with inexpensive small gifts, nuts, candies, and fruits. We also set aside a few days before Christmas for baking our traditional cookies and candies, not only for the family but for neighbors and friends. This emphasizes to our children the spirit of giving. As Ryan says, "I love Christmas because everyone in the neighborhood is always sharing."

Then comes the special night when we go as a family to pick out the Christmas tree. I look for a fir with the best shape, and Jim looks for the best price! Having made the selection, we designate an evening to add the decorations. Excitement fills the room as the lights are strung on the tree and we begin hanging red balls and dozens of specially selected ornaments that I have collected over the years. The house resounds with traditional Christmas music, and we drink hot chocolate and munch our home-baked Christmas cookies and candies. (Is it any wonder that Christmas is such a fattening time in the Dobson household?)

When our children were younger they each had their own "tree"—a small artificial fir which they decorated with lights and their own ornaments. They have become much too sophisticated to continue the tradition, but their memories of the occasion are still warm and meaningful.

On Christmas Eve, we enjoy dinner of Chinese food each year. (Don't ask me how that tradition started, or more important, why?) Afterwards, grandparents, aunts, uncles, and cousins join us around the fireplace, and Jim reads from the Bible. After discussing the passage, we do something very meaningful. The lights are lowered and I give each family member a votive candle. I explain as we take our turn igniting our candle that the light represents Jesus who was born into a dark world to give us eternal life. As each person lights his candle, he shares one blessing he is especially thankful for during the past year, and something he or she is asking God to do in his life the following year—perhaps a spiritual goal for the coming year. We then blow out our candles and

Jim closes in prayer. The children then get to select and open one gift from under the tree.

On Christmas morning, Danae and Ryan open the small gifts in their stockings first; then we have our traditional Christmas brunch, consisting of warm cinnamon rolls, orange juice, and coffee. When the big moment arrives, we sit around the tree, and Ryan and Danae act as "Santa," passing out presents which are opened one at a time in an effort to preserve this happy moment as long as possible.

Finally, we gather at the dining table for our Christmas dinner of turkey, dressing, cranberry sauce, mashed potatoes, two kinds of salads, and hot baked rolls. When we think we can't hold another bite, our traditional dessert of pound cake and ambrosia (a fruit dish prepared with peeled grapes in it) is brought out. The family peels the grapes the evening before the meal. There's always laughter and warm family interaction during this activity. (The recipe for our ambrosia is provided on the opposite page, as well as the recipe for our traditional Christmas brunch cinnamon rolls.)

These happy days of Christmas come and go so quickly that we have sought a way to hold on to the pleasure a while longer. Therefore, we have developed a custom of saving our Christmas cards from friends and loved ones far and wide, and after New Year's Day, I put them on a tray near the dinner table. Every night we select four cards, one for each family member, and we read them and the enclosed letters. We then pray for those families around our table. This tradition may take months to complete, depending on the number of cards we receive. With the busy days of Christmas behind us, we can better enjoy the beauty of the cards, and absorb the meaningful verses and personal notes.

The Christmas traditions that we have developed through the years are not unique to the Dobson household. Perhaps yours are similar in many respects. But they are extremely meaningful to each member of our family. These activities serve to emphasize the two vitally important themes that embody the Christmas spirit: celebration of Jesus' birth and life, and celebration of love for one another and for the entire human family. As such, this exciting time of the year brings out the very best that is within us.

CHRISTMAS MORNING BRUNCH
CINNAMON ROLLS (Serves 6)

1 pkg. Pillsbury Crescent Dinner
  Rolls
  butter or margarine
  granulated sugar
  cinnamon
1 small pkg. crushed pecans

Unroll dough into 4 rectangles (*do not* tear apart as in making crescent dinner rolls). Butter each rectangle generously. Then sprinkle on lots of sugar. Shake cinnamon on top. Add pecans. Roll into small logs and put in refrigerator for 3 minutes. Take out and slice into ¼-inch thick pinwheels. Place on ungreased baking sheet, tucking pinwheel end under roll to prevent its unraveling while baking. Bake according to package instructions. Remove from oven and glaze. Make any powdered sugar glaze to spoon on top while rolls are still warm. Absolutely scrumptious with hot coffee or chocolate, crisp bacon, and scrambled eggs. Merry eating!

AMBROSIA (serves 8)

1 large bunch of green grapes
4-6 large oranges
1 large can crushed pineapple
1 cup chopped pecans
3-4 bananas
1 cup granulated sugar
  whipping cream

Cut each grape in half. Take out seeds and peel off skin. (The men can do this around the table while the women are preparing the meal.) Cut peeling off oranges. Section orange slices and remove all white membrane. Cut each section of orange "meat" in half. Each chunk of orange should be about ¼ inch. Add pineapple, pecans, sliced bananas, and sugar. Mix well. This should be real juicy. Serve in glass dessert dishes with sweetened whipping cream on top. We serve Christmas Ambrosia with pound cake—deelicious!

CHRISTMAS GIFT IDEAS

- A rustic basket or wooden box (cheese or fruit box) lined with a colorful old-fashioned print and filled with spools of thread in basic colors, bias tape, straight pins, needles, a thimble, seam ripper, tape measure, buttons in basic sizes.

- A handmade glasses case (leather, felt, needlepoint), filled with cleaning solution for glasses, Sight-Savers, glasses repair kit.

- A bundle of extra long cinnamon sticks tied with a red and green plaid ribbon and a sprig of holly.

- A carpenter's extra long tape measure, a level, and a square (be sure metric measurements are included).

- A basket filled with shoe polish in basic colors, silicone protecting spray, shoeshine brush and cloth, shoestrings.

- A stocking full of stockings; knee-sox for girls, athletic socks for boys, panty-hose for women, dress socks for men. Tie stocking shut with a bright ribbon.

- A small tin tub lined with straw. Inside the tub pack a glass of homemade jelly and a matching glass containing a homemade spicy candle. A square of gingham tied with ribbon over the top of each jar will add color and personality.

- Several large bars of Ivory soap, a small craft knife, and a booklet on soap carving.

- A whole set of toothbrushes and toothpastes—one for each member of the family. (Be sure each person gets a different color brush.) These may be packed in a small shoebox wrapped in solid color paper. Cut a big smile from red and white paper to put on the top of the box, or paint a smile directly on the box.

- A set of metric wrenches.

GIFT OF TIME

• Each person gives a "gift of time" to every other member of the family. For example: a boy could offer to vacuum the carpet for his mom on the day of her choice; or a father could promise to take his son fishing at some future time.

• Write these time pledges on 3" x 5" cards and place them in envelopes for each person. The envelopes can then be hung on the Christmas tree and opened with the other gifts.

A PRESENT OF PRAISE

• Place a bookmark in the Bible where the Christmas story begins—Luke 2:1-20.

• Give each member of the family a pencil and sheet of paper. (Small children may color a picture.)

• Write (or color) a letter of praise and thanksgiving to Jesus, sharing from the heart. Place the letters with the Bible in a box and wrap as a Christmas present to be opened and shared on Christmas Eve.

CHRISTMAS "WISH BOOK"

• Give your child a mail order catalog and two crayons of different colors.

• Let the child look through the pages for gifts he or she "wishes" to find under the Christmas tree. Use one color to mark first choice and another for second choice with gifts of similar type.

KEEPING THE SECRET

To keep the contents of a package secret, place the wrapped and properly tagged package inside a larger box. Pad with newspaper or tissue so there will be no rattling. Wrap outer package and label with another person's name. Do this with as many packages as you wish. When packages are unwrapped, the inner gift is given to the right person to open. Everyone will enjoy *both* surprises! (If you do not want to have to wrap two packages, try making a "quiet" package noisy by adding a few buttons or dried beans, or a light package heavy by adding a rock or other heavy object.)

MAKING CHRISTMAS EVE MEMORIES

Adapt any or all of the following to make a tradition of Christmas Eve for your family:

- Take a drive through town or a nearby large city to see the outdoor light displays.

- Read the Christmas story aloud from the Bible.

- Sing carols around the piano or sing with a favorite Christmas record.

- Have every family member take his turn giving some kind of Christmas performance.

- Attend a candlelight or watch night service. Make attending this special service an annual family affair.

- Let the children open one gift on Christmas Eve. (Perhaps this gift could be sleep wear to keep the children snuggly and warm on Christmas Eve.)

- Hang stockings (to be filled after children are asleep with such things as small toys, toothbrush, comb or brush, old-fashioned toys such as kaleidoscope, wooden top, jacks, pickup sticks, wooden flute, whistle, etc.)

- Serve hot wassail. A suggested recipe follows.

HOT WASSAIL

- In the base of a twelve-cup percolator put:

    1 part cranapple juice
    5 parts apple cider
      (unpasteurized)

- In the percolator basket put:

    6-8 whole cloves
    2 cinnamon sticks
    2 tbsp. honey
    ¼ chopped lemon including rind

- Brew wassail as you normally would coffee.

- Serve hot with a sliver of lemon or a cinnamon stick.

NOTE: If the family condones belief in Santa, the children could make a snack to leave out for him. Another nice tradition might be for Mom and Dad to have a glass of eggnog together after the children are in bed and take time to talk about love, blessings, goals, etc., or just enjoy a few quiet moments with each other.

MAKING CHRISTMAS MORNING EXTRA SPECIAL

- Take pictures of the children getting up on Christmas morning.

- Have the children stay in bed until Dad gives a special signal. (He could put a record on the stereo such as "Here Comes Santa Claus" or some other Christmas music.)

- Race to be the first to yell out some special phrase: "Christmas gift!" or "Merry Christmas!"

- Have a short worship time before opening gifts. Children could do this with parents being the "congregation."

- Have a special Christmas breakfast every year. A sample menu might include: fried apples, grapefruit and eggs; blueberry muffins, scrambled eggs and bacon; or dried beef gravy on homemade biscuits. (Some families serve "chocolate gravy" that is similar to chocolate pudding, but thinner.)

CHRISTMAS DAY REUNION

- Gather the family together for a reunion at grandparents' home. Make it a "bring-in" dinner, everyone supplying his/her special dish, so that no one has all the work!

- Choose one person to be "Santa" and pass out gifts. This might be the same person each time, or the honor could go to the youngest child or the youngest teenager; or, all could "draw straws" for the honor.

- Celebrate by singing around the piano.

- Listen together as Grandfather or other older family member reads the Christmas story, or recite it together from Luke, chapter 2.

- Make plaster-of-Paris hand prints each Christmas season. Paint with bright colors, shellac, or spray with fixative. Put name, year, and age on back. Save from year to year. See instructions on p. 133 for making prints with plaster of Paris.

- Before Christmas dinner, put two fresh cranberries on each plate. After the family is seated, pass around a basket and, as cranberries are dropped in, share two ways in which Christmas is special to you. Follow by reading John 3:16, and conclude with prayer.

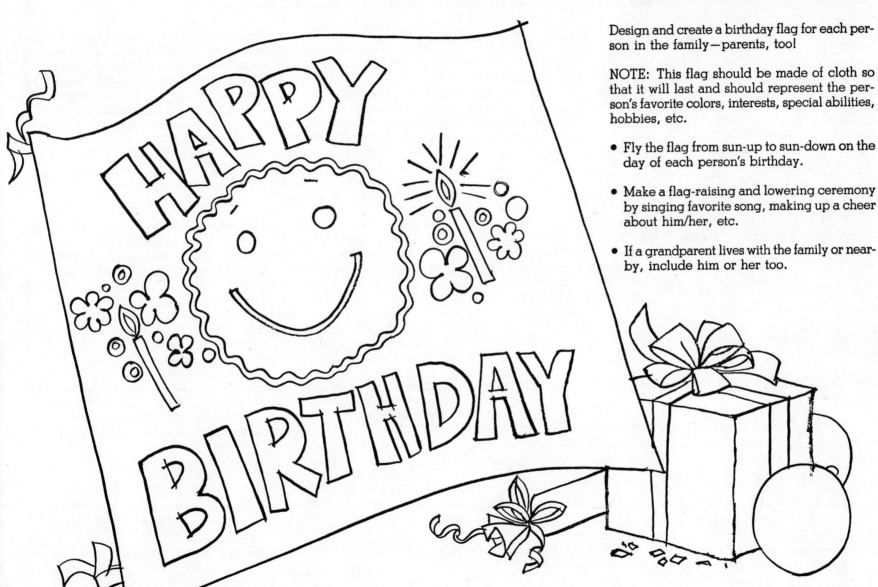

BIRTHDAY FLAG

Design and create a birthday flag for each person in the family—parents, too!

NOTE: This flag should be made of cloth so that it will last and should represent the person's favorite colors, interests, special abilities, hobbies, etc.

- Fly the flag from sun-up to sun-down on the day of each person's birthday.

- Make a flag-raising and lowering ceremony by singing favorite song, making up a cheer about him/her, etc.

- If a grandparent lives with the family or nearby, include him or her too.

SPECIAL DAYS / BIRTHDAYS

RYAN—SUNSHINE OF MY LIFE

"What are little boys made of? Frogs and snails and puppy dog tails . . . that's what little boys are made of."

Thirteen years ago, a little boy named Ryan blessed our home with his presence. He has been a delight and a joy to our family since that moment. His personality radiates happiness in every room of our house, and his energy is boundless. As the evening nears and I begin to wear down, Ryan accelerates his pace and attacks the many activities that captivate his alert mind. Once in a while, I can corner him long enough to give him a hug.

A few years ago during the week of my birthday, our family decided to go for a leisurely stroll through our local shopping center. Ryan was only eight at the time, and he loved to visit the mall. He opened his piggybank and took out $5.00 that he had been saving for something special. As we walked along window shopping and enjoying being together, Ryan announced that he wanted to have some time alone to go to the toy store and pet shop. We set a time and place where we would meet and off he went. In about thirty minutes, he came walking up with a grin that stretched from ear to ear.

Ryan said, "Here, Mom, this is for your birthday—you can open it right now."

I answered, "But, Ryan, it isn't my birthday yet. Can I save it and open it on Friday?"

By the look on his face it was obvious that he felt very strongly about my opening the gift right there in the center of the shopping mall. He announced it cost *a lot* of money (he had spent the entire $5.00 on it). I carefully opened the package and was filled with emotion as I gazed with tenderness on its contents. The gift was not one that you would expect to receive from an eight-year-old boy. He had bought me a lovely desk set. The ostrich-feathered white pen looked like an old fashioned quill that Ben Franklin might have used to sign the Declaration of Independence. The stand was padded in matching white, with a spray of pink flowers delicately painted around the edges. I was so touched that my eyes brimmed with tears as I hugged and thanked my son for such an extravagant gift. It has been five years since that day and the pen still sits on the nightstand near my bed as a reminder of Ryan's spontaneous gift of love.

There are times in our lives when the cost of parenting seems staggeringly high! No matter how you look at it, children are emotionally exhausting, time-consuming, sometimes frustrating, and always maddeningly complex. In fact, their developmental years are governed entirely by "Murphy's Law." For example, if they drop a slice of bread on the carpet, it will inevitably land buttered side down. And when they catch the flu, they *never* vomit in the bathroom. They turn up their noses at their oatmeal and gag at the sight of their eggs, but enthusiastically drink the dog's water and float their rubber duckies in the toilet, etc. I'm sure you could add to this list of childhood "Murphyisms."

But in moments when you are touched by the soul of a child, as I was through Ryan's act of love, you suddenly realize the eternal significance of these precious years. Then, no other task on earth seems quite as important or meaningful as raising and training and guiding him through his developmental experiences.

SPECIAL FROM BEGINNING TO END

- Choose one gift and put it at the birthday person's place at the breakfast table to be opened as soon as his/her day begins.

- Ask the birthday person to plan the menu for supper. Give it to the family at this time so that his/her wishes can be carried out. (Or, let the birthday person choose a favorite eating place, as the budget allows.)

- Make sure the birthday person has fresh clean sheets to sleep on for the birthday night.

ANNUAL BIRTHDAY INTERVIEW

- On each child's birthday, record on cassette tape an interview with him or her. Ask him or her to describe special memories about the past year—happy times, sad moments, fun things that happened, and other meaningful experiences.

- Add to the recording every year at the time of each birthday.

- After each interview, play back the previous years' conversations.

SPECIAL DAYS / BIRTHDAYS

CREATIVE GIFTS

Here are some ideas for very special birthday gifts:

- Tickets to the zoo, a concert, a craft show, a film.

- A prepaid motel reservation for parents of young children (so they can rediscover each other alone).

- A pretty basket containing gardening gloves, small shovel, flower seeds, liquid fertilizer, etc.

- A large roll of Scotch tape for a young child (aged four to seven) who seldom is allowed to have tape to use as he wishes.

- A poem written especially for the "birthday person," perhaps mounted on a pretty piece of wood or written by hand in ink in the front of an "empty book" for writing about special moments all year long. (Available at stationery stores.)

- A cassette tape containing a song or message about the birthday person.

- A set of handmade gingham napkins, colorfully displayed in a bread or cracker basket.

- A basket of fragrant soaps, tied with a ribbon to match the bathroom. (This gift is equally welcomed by men, women, and children. Choose masculine or juvenile soaps and ribbon for men or children.)

- A cassette of the birthday person's baby, child, parent far away, son in service, etc.

- A beach towel.

- A swim mask, nose plugs, swim fins.

- A crockware jug, tin bucket, or wooden pail filled with dried flowers, colorful wash cloths, dish towels, cattails, spices.

- A kerosene lamp with lamp oil, a hand-crocheted table scarf, and an old book from a flea market.

- Two or three colorful belts.

- A stapler and two or three boxes of staples (for kids, too!).

- Art supplies.

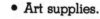

A KID'S FAVORITE

RED RASPBERRY BIRTHDAY CAKE

1 pkg. white cake mix
2 tbsp. flour
1 red raspberry Jell-O, regular size

•

½ cup water
1 cup vegetable oil
4 eggs
1 10-oz. pkg. frozen red
    raspberries, divided

•

1 box confectioner's sugar
1 stick margarine or butter

Mix together the dry cake mix, flour, and raspberry Jell-O. Combine the water and vegetable oil and add to the dry mixture. Add the four eggs one at a time, mixing well. Stir in *half* the frozen red raspberries.

HINT: Cut block of raspberries in half while still frozen so that exactly half can be saved for icing.

Pour batter into three greased and floured 8-in. layer cake pans. Bake at 325 degrees for 20 minutes or until cake feels bouncy in the center.

For icing, combine the softened butter or margarine, confectioner's sugar, and reserved half of the raspberries, thawed. Mix together with electric mixer. Spread on cooled cake.

SPECIAL DAYS / BIRTHDAYS

SPECIAL BIRTHDAY PARTIES

"DO-IT-YOURSELF" BIRTHDAY PARTY

- Plan a birthday party for six or eight children, ages ten and younger.

- Look in your cookbook for a yummy gingerbread cookie recipe and assemble the ingredients needed to make it, along with the necessary utensils.

- When the guests arrive, let them help you make gingerbread boy cookies. Each child can then take home the cookie he made.

ADOPTED BIRTHDATE

- Celebrate an "extra" birthday on the date your adopted son/daughter came to be your child. The attention he receives on that day is designed to make him know his adoption was a blessed event to be celebrated rather than a dark secret to be hidden. This second birthday makes adopted children feel special.

INSTANT PARTY FOR A LOVED ONE AWAY FROM HOME

- Bake cookies and arrange them in a box with packets of fruit punch mix, party napkins, and paper cups.

- Wrap the box in birthday paper with a card explaining that you are sending an "instant party."

- Finish with an outer wrapping of brown paper and mail to that special birthday person.

HAPPY "HALF" BIRTHDAY

- On each child's "half" birthday, have a half celebration: at age two and a half, three and a half, etc.

- Bake a "half" cake and serve a half glass of punch. Give the child money for half a toy and let him earn the other half. He will be delightfully surprised.

THE GIFT OF WHAT YOU ARE

- Buy large empty capsules from drugstore or pharmacy.

- On strips of bright paper, have each member of the family write "I love you because . . ." and sign his/her name on the back. Each person may contribute as many as he wishes.

- Roll strips tightly and insert in capsule.

- Put capsules in small box (jewelry container or match box) and wrap or decorate box.

- Give to the birthday person to read now or to save for special "low" days. Great medicine to counteract discouragement all year long!

NOTE: This gift is very special for someone away at college or in the service.

SPECIAL DAYS / BIRTHDAYS

BAKED POTATO SUPPER

- Wrap large potatoes in aluminum foil and bake them in the oven about one hour at 350 degrees. Time the baking so the potatoes are just done when everyone arrives.

- Prepare all kinds of trappings and set them out buffet style so that everyone can fix his or her own potato.

  two or three kinds of grated cheese
  chives
  crumbled bacon
  chopped green peppers
  chopped onion
  cooked and drained hamburger bits
  cooked and drained sausage bits
  sliced ripe olives
  sour cream
  butter
  chopped peanuts
  sunflower seeds

- Serve cold drinks and coffee or iced tea.

GOD'S DAY IS SPECIAL

- Celebrate the Day of Worship with a special tablecloth or placemats used at breakfast or lunch and *only* on that day.

- The mats can be sewn by Mom, or the children can make their own from construction paper and colorfully decorate them with crayons or marker pens.

- This tradition will help the family recognize that the Day of Worship is special because it is God's Day.

SPECIAL DAY TOYS

- Choose or buy five or six toys or games that delight a child.

- Save these to be used or played with only on the Lord's Day.

- Since there is more time to enjoy each other on this day, make a special effort to play with your child and his/her special toys and games.

SPECIAL DAY MUSIC

- Use music to make the Day of Worship special by playing only Christian or classical music on this day.

- Sing a familiar chorus, hymn, or verse together as a grace for dinner on the Day of Worship.

- Read the history of a familiar hymn as part of the family worship. Then sing the hymn together.

- Make this a treat by also doing special things together as a family while music is playing, for example:

  - Make chocolate chip cookies.

  - Play Scrabble, Boggle, or other word games.

  - Paint or sculpt.

  - Do a huge jigsaw puzzle.

  - Play the music together on the various instruments your family plays.

SPECIAL DAYS / DAY OF WORSHIP

SPECIAL SUPPER

If the main meal on the Day of Worship is at noon, have the suppertime or evening after-church snack be a prepared-by-Dad special. Try the following idea for a starter:

DAD'S CHEESE MELTS

- Start with slices of buttered crunchy wheat bread and mild Colby cheese.

- Melt cheese on bread in oven until cheese is bubbly.

- Serve on paper plates with chunks of dill pickle and glasses of cold milk.

SAND DOLLAR REMEMBRANCE

- When someone becomes a Christian and receives Jesus into his life, commemorate the occasion by giving him or her a sand dollar (any object can be substituted).

- Place it in a prominent place such as on a nightstand, kitchen counter, window ledge, etc..

- As a remembrance of this special occasion, date the object with a waterproof pen.

- Each year on the anniversary of the date, bring attention to that important decision with a special prayer before dinner.

- For another remembrance of this important event, take a photograph of the person on his/her day of decision. Document the relevant information on the back of the picture.

SPECIAL DAYS / DAY OF WORSHIP

BLACK SUNDAY

The following article appeared originally in my husband's book, *Straight Talk to Men and Their Wives,* and is adapted here with permission of Word, Incorporated.

Is Sunday morning a particularly difficult time in your home? For some reason, the Sabbath can be the most frustrating day of the week for our family, especially during the "get 'em ready for church" routine. But Black Sunday was uniquely chaotic! We began that day by getting up too late, meaning everyone had to rush to get to church on time. That produced emotional pressure, especially for Jim and me. Then there was the matter of spilled milk at breakfast, and the black shoe polish on the floor. And, of course, Ryan got dressed first, enabling him to slip out the back door and get himself dirty from head to toe. It was necessary to take him down to the skin and start over with clean clothes once more. Instead of handling these irritants as they arose, we began criticizing one another and hurling accusations back and forth. At least one spanking was delivered, as I recall, and another three or four were promised. Yes, it was a day to be remembered (or forgotten). Finally, four harried people managed to stumble into church, ready for a great spiritual blessing, no doubt. There's not a pastor in the world who could have moved us on that morning.

I felt guilty throughout the day for the strident tone of our home on that Black Sunday. Sure, our children shared the blame, but they were merely responding to our disorganization. We had overslept, and that's where the conflict originated.

After the evening service, we called the family together around the kitchen table. We began by describing the kind of day we had had, and asked each person to forgive us for our part in it. Furthermore, we said that we thought we should give each member of the family an opportunity to say whatever he or she was feeling inside.

Ryan was given the first shot, and he fired it at me. "You've been a real grouch today, Mom!" he said with feeling. "You've blamed me for everything I've done all day long."

I then explained why I had been unhappy with him, trying not to be defensive about his charges.

Danae then poured out her hostilities and frustrations. Finally, Jim and I had an opportunity to explain the tensions that had caused our over-reaction.

It was a valuable time of ventilation and honesty that drew us together once more. We then had prayer as a family and asked the Lord to help us live and work together in love and harmony.

Every family has moments when they violate all the rules—even departing from the Christian principles by which they have lived. Fatigue itself can damage all the high ideals which have been recommended to parents in seminars, books and sermons. The important question is, how do mothers and fathers reestablish friendship within their families when the storm has passed? Open, non-threatening discussion offers one solution to that situation.

FAMILY NIGHT*

Designate one evening a week as family night. If you have a special activity such as roller skating that the whole family enjoys doing together, you might plan to do that on the night you have chosen.

Try to make family night the same day every week so that every family member will keep that night free when making individual plans.

If you don't have special plans for family night, bring out the fun box.

HOW TO MAKE A FUN BOX

- Get a box; a shoebox or empty round oatmeal box is the best.

- Decorate the outside together, labeling the box "Family Fun Box."

- Have each family member write down on slips of paper something to do as a family. These activities could include:

  bowling
  reading a book aloud
  seeing a movie
  sending out for pizza
  going for a bike ride

- When the designated evening rolls around, pull a slip of paper from the fun box and do whatever it tells you.

- Replenish the slips of paper either by replacing the slip just drawn or by adding to the box as family members come up with additional ideas.

*See list of Resources for Family Reading and Activities on p. 220.

SPECIAL DAYS / ORDINARY DAYS

THE MAGIC HOUR*

If you have children of school age, make it a rule for one parent to be home when the children arrive home from school.

This is the moment for maximum communication. . . .

HINTS

- Do baking at this hour or just before so that the house always smells wonderful—like someone's there who loves you!

- Play music that denotes joy and peace.

- Have nutritious snacks ready as a convenient option to junk foods—carrot and celery sticks, sunflower seeds and raisins, orange juice.

- Be prepared to listen enthusiastically.

- Give at least half-an-hour "wind-down" time before requiring practice of musical instruments, homework, or chores.

- Try to discourage television at this hour by having more interesting options.

*Special thanks to Joyce Landorf for sharing this "memory maker" with us.

TOGETHERNESS

HOMEWORK

- Work is always more fun when loved ones do it together. Sit down with your children during their homework hour and use this time to answer correspondence, work on the family album, or catch up on the mending. The children will concentrate better, and parents will be there to answer any questions that might arise.

- A time of play (a table game or a walk around the block) is an ideal follow-up to the time of shared discipline.

TEEN TALK

As a teenager's schedule becomes more hectic, it is important to make time for parent and child to keep talking together. Here are some ways to save time for each other:

- Save the last fifteen minutes before bedtime to share together in the teenager's room. A middle-of-the-bed picnic of popcorn or peanuts and a beverage can be a special treat as you talk about the day. ("Tucking in" time is not just for young children.) This is a good time to read a verse of Scripture or page from a devotional book together, with the teenager, not the parent, doing the choosing and reading.

- An out-of-town, one-day vacation or shopping spree is a good time to talk. At times this may warrant getting the teenager out of school for a special day, especially if it is a high-stress time. Sometimes kids need a break, too. (The parent should not take another adult along to talk to, but should just delight in the company of this child who is becoming an adult and a new friend.)

- Save Sundays. Try not to overschedule the "Lord's Day," but keep it free for family time. Parents who honor this day can more easily expect growing children to save this time. Be ready to listen to good music, do art projects, take walks, etc.

- Biking and hiking provide good opportunities for communication, especially between one parent and one teenager at a time. Other times it's fun to have the whole family.

- Be spontaneous. A fish fry at midnight, a breakfast in the park, a surprise lunch date away from school, a surprise gift when it's nobody's birthday, a special privilege—all these can open the door for real communication.

- Take lessons together—horseback riding, archery, tennis, basket weaving, ceramics, skiing, cake decorating—or take up a new interest like drag racing, fishing, tennis, skeet shooting, mountain climbing, dress designing. Often the teenager will excel and have the new experience of helping a parent master the new skill.

- Keep on hugging and touching. It is a terrible shock to children to have the hugging stop just at the age when they need it most. Avoid saying, "You're too old for that." Let teenagers cry, giggle, sit on your lap, kiss you good-night, or talk into the wee hours of the morning.

SPECIAL DAYS / ORDINARY DAYS

CONVERSATIONAL TENNIS

- Supply yourself with half a dozen or more tennis balls.

- Ask your elementary school child to sit on a chair on the opposite side of the room from you.

- Throw him a tennis ball, but ask him to catch it and hold it in his lap. Then toss him another and another.

- Sit and look at one another for a few moments until he asks you to explain your point.

- Then say, "It isn't much of a game until you throw the balls back to me, is it?" Continue to show him how conversation is also a game that requires people to toss their ideas back and forth. Explain that if you merely "catch" the other person's comment, but don't return it with one of your own, that's like holding the tennis balls in your lap; it ruins the fun.

- Practice "tossing" words back and forth with your child. You may say, for example, "Did you have a good day in school?" If the child says, "Yeah," in return, he has merely caught your words. But if he says, "Yes, I got an A in math," he has learned to throw you a comment of his own.

- Discuss how well the child returns adult comments the next time he plays conversational tennis with friends and associates.

PLAY TOGETHER

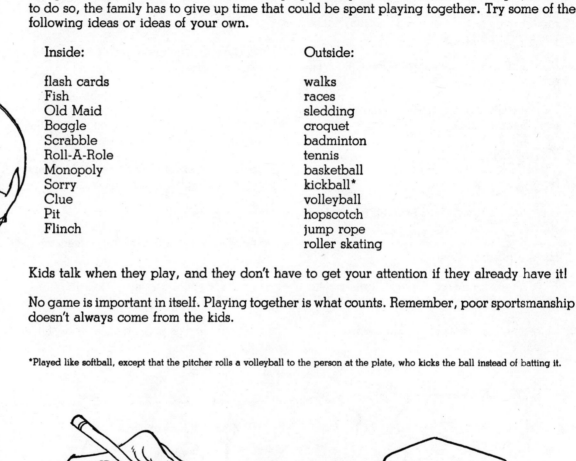

Use your children as a wonderful excuse to play! Hardly ever is TV worth watching if, in order to do so, the family has to give up time that could be spent playing together. Try some of the following ideas or ideas of your own.

Inside:	Outside:
flash cards	walks
Fish	races
Old Maid	sledding
Boggle	croquet
Scrabble	badminton
Roll-A-Role	tennis
Monopoly	basketball
Sorry	kickball*
Clue	volleyball
Pit	hopscotch
Flinch	jump rope
	roller skating

Kids talk when they play, and they don't have to get your attention if they already have it!

No game is important in itself. Playing together is what counts. Remember, poor sportsmanship doesn't always come from the kids.

*Played like softball, except that the pitcher rolls a volleyball to the person at the plate, who kicks the ball instead of batting it.

SPECIAL DAYS / ORDINARY DAYS

INSTEAD OF TV

Tonight instead of watching TV, try doing one of the following together as a family:

- Model objects out of clay. (You may make your own. See page 85.)

- Make collages of seeds, grains, cereal, paper scraps.

- Take a walk (maybe a drive to the woods or park before dark).

- Play badminton.

- Sing old songs.

- Have an everybody-do-something talent show.

- Have a puppet show.

- Have a read-aloud (each person gets to read or have his/her favorite poem or story read).

- Light candles and play old records.

- Catch fireflies.

- Have devotions outdoors on a porch, deck, patio, or sunroof.

- Have a bonfire and roast marshmallows.

- Redecorate all the bulletin boards in the house. (Choose teams for each board.)

- Make Valentines (or Christmas cards, wrapping paper, jack-o-lanterns, etc.)

- Make popcorn balls.

- Do needlework, latch-hook rugs, macramé, etc.

- Play Carom, Ping-Pong, pick-up-sticks, jacks, tiddlywinks. (Dad, too!)

- String cranberries, popcorn, Cheerios, Lifesavers.

RECIPES FOR FUN

Simple crafts to do at home provide marvelous opportunities for children to develop creativity while at the same time enjoying the togetherness of working with Mom or Dad or an older brother or sister.

HOMEMADE PASTE

1 cup flour
½ cup water

Combine and mix until creamy. Store in covered container. This paste can be used for paper crafts or papier-mâché.

HOMEMADE FINGER PAINT

Mix equal parts of paste (made from recipe above) and liquid detergent and add food coloring. Or, add food coloring to liquid starch.

HINT: The best paper to use for finger painting is shelf paper, shiny banquet-table paper or butcher paper. Paper should be dipped in water before applying paint. Try finger painting with toes, elbows, knees, fists, bits of sponge. (Chocolate pudding also makes great finger paint . . . and it's okay to taste the paint!)

YARN ART "STAINED GLASS"

- Cut several lengths (12–24 inches) of brightly colored yarn.

- Cover table or counter area with newspapers.

- Mix in a bowl:

    2 tbsp. white glue
    2 tbsp. water

- Soak the yarn in the glue; then squeeze through fingers to remove excess glue.

- Press yarn pieces to brightly colored tissue paper, creating the desired design.

- Allow to dry thoroughly.

- Trim tissue from edges.

- Hang designs in front of a window or use shapes to create a mobile. Seasonal shapes may be made if desired.

CORNSTARCH AND SODA CLAY

This clay can be molded into shapes and vessels, or rolled on waxed paper and cut with cookie cutters. When dry, it can be painted.

NOTE: This mixture is *not* to be eaten, but is intended for crafts only.

Ingredients:

    2 cups baking soda
    1 cup cornstarch
    1¼ cups cold water

- Combine all ingredients in saucepan until smooth.

- Bring to boil and boil one minute, stirring until clay is the consistency of mashed potatoes.

- Pour out onto a tray and cover with damp cloth until cool.

- Knead lightly (knead in a few drops of food coloring, if desired).

- Use immediately or store, wrapped air-tight, in refrigerator. Warm to room temperature before using.

SPECIAL DAYS / ORDINARY DAYS

SPIN A LITTLE LOVE

- Have the family sit in a circle on the floor of the family room or den.

- Take turns spinning a bottle and telling something positive about the family member to whom the bottle points. Express the love message directly to the person rather than to the entire group.

- Go around the circle one more time and share events, surprises, or matters of interest which happened in that day.

FOR A SPECIAL PERSON

A BREAKFAST DATE

- Choose one person in the family at a time for an early breakfast date.

- Include each child and your wife or husband.

- Let the date choose the place, or surprise him/her with some little nook you've lately discovered.

- Get up and leave early enough so that there is time to enjoy the dawn and eat and talk without a great deal of rushing.

- If it is a Saturday date, perhaps this would be a good chance to visit an elderly relative afterward. Give your child the gift of real friendship with people of *all* ages.

HONOR PLATE

- Choose an unusual or attractively colored plate to be used *only* on a special occasion.*

- Serve a meal on that plate when a member of the family is to be honored, such as on Father's Day, Mother's Day, a birthday, after receiving a good report card or an award, or after a difficult job is finished, etc.

- The honor plate is then washed and put away until the next "celebration" day.

HONOR FLAG

- Let each child design his/her own flag, and then help in its creation.

- Fly the flag on any special day for that individual when the honor plate is being used.

*For information on how to order a unique "You're Something Special" plate, see p. 223.

SPECIAL DAYS / ORDINARY DAYS

THE DINNER HOUR

Try to make dinner a special occasion every day, even if you have small children. Try to include the following every evening:

- A centerpiece on the table. (This can be live or dried flowers, a basket of vegetables, a few stones and a piece of driftwood, a small limb of colorful leaves; anything that brings nature to the table.)

- Candles, lighted!

- Place-settings with napkins and real dishes—never paper.

Just as important as the physical setting is the pleasantness of the mealtime. Try to observe the following ground rules:

- Food that is nutritious, balanced, colorful, and delicious. (Even simple meals can be served with pizazz!)

- Good conversation about the day from each person and encouragement offered from all.

- Soft music that is soothing to the nerves.

- No disciplining or heavy correcting of children.

- No fighting, whining, yelling, etc.

- "No-knock policy" is in effect for the thirty to forty-five minutes of mealtime. Nobody can say anything (even sarcastically or jokingly) to hurt another family member.

PUZZLE PLACE

When things are rushed or hectic, or when there are a lot of guests in and out, set out a huge 500-piece puzzle on the coffee table or game table

- Don't worry about the clutter. Just leave the puzzle out.

- Don't be surprised if guests who might otherwise be timid are drawn to the puzzle.

- Watch how many good conversations are precipitated by this simple-to-share task.

- Don't be surprised if kids are the best puzzle-solvers!

SPECIAL DAYS / ORDINARY DAYS

SPECIAL DAYS / ORDINARY DAYS

TAKE NOTE

Get into the habit of writing notes to persons in the family. A memo board in the kitchen is a good place to write notes, or:

- Put a note in a child's or father's lunch box.

- Slip a note in a geometry book or flute case.

- Leave a note on the mirror Dad will use when he shaves.

- Tie a note to the steering wheel of the car, truck, or tractor.

- Pin a note to the pillow when making the bed.

- Put a note on each person's plate before the dinner hour.

A note is a good way to say:

- "I'm glad I have you for a sister."

- "Thanks for always fixing such yummy meals."

- "Have a good day! I'll be praying for you during your math test."

- "As you drive to work, whistle, 'You Are Loved.' "

- "I just thought of five things I'm thankful for, and they all live in this house!"

Save special notes you've received. What a treasure they will be someday!

MAKING MEMORIES THROUGH THE SEASONS

SEASONS / SPRING

THE SPRING RUSH

Before spring actually arrives, watch for its promises. When the snow is still on the ground in late February or early March:

• Pick limbs of pussy willows and bring them inside. Put them in water and watch spring pop out!

• Pick forsythia at the first sign of budding, and bring it in.

• Plant tulip, daffodil, or hyacinth bulbs inside. Keep them watered and in a sunny window.

• Fill the house with construction paper daisies. Tape them to windows, doors, refrigerator, or hang them with black thread from ceiling lights, etc.

• Welcome the birds with suet, tiny balls of meat, and seeds.

• Cut off the tops of milk cartons. Fill the cartons with soil and plant dwarf marigold seeds. They come up and grow quickly, and they may even be ready to bloom by the time it's warm enough to transplant them outside.

SPRING FIRSTS

Use a bulletin board or chalkboard in a prominent place to record spring firsts.

- Print or letter the title "SPRING FIRSTS" at the top of the board.

- As a family, discuss the things that remind each person of a typical spring sight. Then decide on the things everyone should be on the lookout for and list them under the title on the board.

- The first person to spot a first sign of spring gets to put his/her name on the board beside the appropriate spring first, along with a picture of what was observed.

FIRST ROBIN CONTEST

Make a separate, yearly contest of any one of the ideas from the Spring Firsts above.

- After a cold eastern or midwestern winter, it's especially appealing to welcome spring by having a "first robin" contest. The first member of the family to see and report a robin is the winner.

- This contest can continue even after children are grown. No matter where they are, they can call home with "first robin" and claim the victory. This tradition represents the triumphant return of spring.

SPRING FIRSTS
- A ROBIN — MINDY
- PINKISH BLOOM ON MAPLE TREE — TED
- GREEN GRASS THROUGH THE SNOW — MOM
- KIDS ON SKATES — DAD

SEASONS / SPRING

SPRINGTIME FUN

Here are two activities that are especially good for elementary and preschool aged children. But be prepared to have their older brothers and sisters want to join in too!

SPRING PENNY WALK

- When the flowers and trees begin to bloom, take a "Spring Penny Walk" to enjoy the beautiful sights of spring.

- Toss a penny at each intersection to determine what path will be taken on the tour. Heads indicates a right turn and tails specifies a left turn. Enjoy the excitement of finding where "luck" takes you.

- After arriving back home, have each member of the family color a picture of what he or she likes best about spring.

- Share the pictures at dinnertime.

VEGETABLE POT GARDEN

Children love to eat what they grow.

- Put each child's name on a pot along with the name of the vegetable he/she will plant in it.

- Fill the pots with rich soil and plant a few vegetable seeds, such as carrots, radishes, or beans. Watching it grow from a tiny seed is fascinating for a young child.

- When the vegetable is harvested and prepared, put the child's name on the serving dish that contains it: Jim's Corn, Sherrie's Tomatoes, Nancy's Carrots.

BLOSSOM FESTIVAL

When the fruit blossoms first appear, have a family blossom festival. The following activities might be included:

- Decorate windows and bulletin boards with pictures drawn or cut from magazines (seed catalogs and garden magazines are best) of the fruit that is most commonly grown in your area: apple, peach, orange, cherry.

- Bring in dead limbs and decorate them with mock blossoms made from tissue or crepe paper.

- Make ice cream using frozen fruit from last year's crop.

- Celebrate the bees. Point out that without them there would be no fruit. Ask one child to find out why, and make a report at the supper table.

- Tie big "welcome ribbons" around each budding tree in the color of the fruit that the tree will bear. For example, use red or burgundy ribbons for cherries, peach for peaches, and gold for pears.

- Make garlands for the girls to wear on their heads. These can be made of floral wire or craft chenille wire, tissue blossoms, and leaves.

- Plant a seedling together. If your yard is small, a dwarf tree is best. For specific instructions, see p. 155. You may want to use this idea in the fall to allow time for the seedling to develop a root system during the dormant winter months.

SEASONS / SPRING

MAY DAY MORNING SURPRISE

- On May 1, get up before anyone else in the family.

- Go outside and pick a bouquet of spring flowers (daffodils, tulips, or whatever is in bloom in your area).

- Put them in a pretty basket that can hang on a doorknob. If you like, make your own basket from the instructions below.

- Go to the house of someone you want to surprise. Hang the May basket on the knob of the front door. Ring the doorbell and then hide behind the shrubbery or around the corner of the house.

- When someone comes to the door, jump out and yell, "May Day!"

MAY DAY BASKET

- Fold a sheet of construction paper diagonally.

- Cut off the bottom of sheet to form a square. Save this piece to make a handle.

- Roll and glue side and bottom edge to form a cone shape.

- Cut two strips from discarded piece and glue them together. Then glue one end of the long strip to each side of cone to form a handle.

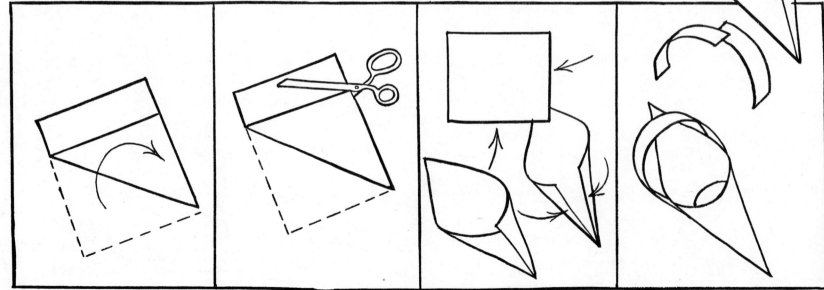

LAST DAY OF SCHOOL

Make it a tradition to do something special for the last day of school, such as:

- Go out for breakfast as soon as report cards have been picked up.

- Have the season's first bike hike.

- Tie "Welcome Summer" streamers across the doorway.

- Go swimming. Have a pool opening party or go to the nearest public swimming pool.

- Buy some sandals.

- Celebrate the last day of school and the beginning of summer with *special* cookies (see Summer Lollipop Cookies described below) and lemonade.

SUMMER LOLLIPOP COOKIES

- Use a favorite crispy cookie recipe.

- Roll out the dough (not too thin) and cut it into round shapes with a cookie cutter or glass.

- Place the cookies on a baking sheet and insert a wooden popsicle stick one or two inches into the base of each circle.

- After baking, and after the cookies have cooled, frost them with a sunshine-yellow icing.

- Let each cookie represent the summer sun. Candies or raisins can be used to decorate the "sun" with creative faces.

- Serve with iced lemonade.

SEASONS / SUMMER

SUMMER MEMORY BOOK

- Starting at the beginning of summer, record dates of special outings, family activities, unusual events, etc. Paste or tape into the notebook ticket stubs, programs, place cards or other souvenirs that will fit into the notebook.

- Record the height and weight of each member of the family.

- At the end of the season look back on the activities of the summer and enjoy the memories you have created.

MATERIALS NEEDED

Large spiral notebook or scrapbook
Paper
Marker pens or crayons
Glue
Scotch tape
Measuring tape
Scales for weighing

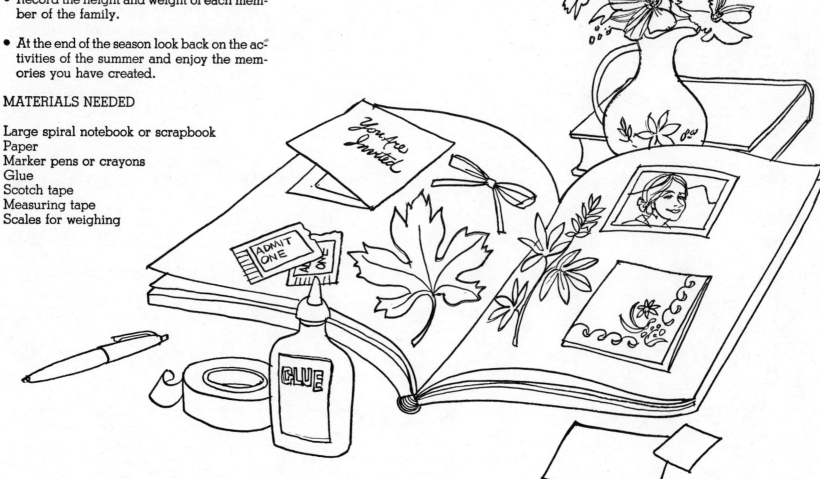

SUMMER EXCURSIONS

BEACH DAY

Throughout the summer, select one day each week—preferably the same day—for a family outing. Take the children to the beach, on a picnic, or on some other outdoor activity. Keeping this a regularly scheduled time will give the children something to look forward to and count on as their special time. Try not to combine this time with business or other social engagements, but keep it as a time for family only.

BERRY PICKING

Go as a family to pick berries together. The following checklist might be helpful:

- Be sure to wear clothing to cover arms and legs; blackberry and raspberry bushes are prickly.

- Take containers for each person.

- Choose old, comfortable clothes and shoes.

- Adults or older children might share some of their berries with the smaller persons. It's more fun when it "looks like ya got more."

- Plan something special afterward, like eating ice cream cones or drinking ice-cold lemonade.

- Have everyone help with the stemming and cleaning when you get home. Somehow, cooperation makes the berries taste even better.

- Freeze the berries you are not going to use right away. They can be frozen without sugar. Spread the washed, drained berries on a cookie sheet, and place it directly onto a shelf in the freezer. After the berries are frozen, scoop them into storage bags and return them to the freezer.

BICYCLE BREAKFAST

- Assemble the whole family early on a summer morning around six o'clock.

- Pack a simple breakfast that can be carried in bike baskets:

  individual cereals
  plastic spoons
  Thermos of milk (or unopened cartons)
  Thermos of coffee
  plastic bag of fruit (e.g., apple, orange and pineapple slices, grapes, raisins)
  plastic bag of bran or fruit muffins
  blanket or plastic tablecloth
  small Bible (eternal nourishment)

- Ride to the country on bikes. Get permission ahead of time to visit someone's woods, or go to the park or beach.

- Spread the blanket or tablecloth to sit on. Take time to comment on lovely things; keep conversation happy, observant, and thoughtful.

- Read together a short psalm of praise.

- After breakfast, let the children gather wild flowers or just run and play.

SEASONS / SUMMER

GALLERY THREE

- Gather together all of the crafts and similar items the family has made throughout the summer:

    jewelry
    rock sculpture
    yarn art
    collages
    paintings

- Make some lemonade and brownies.

- Sell your treasures at a "roadside" stand or a neighborhood craft sale.

- To make the project more meaningful, plan to donate some of the proceeds to homeless refugees from the Third World, a community relief project, or a family who recently lost their home in a fire, etc.

NEIGHBORHOOD ART SHOW

AHEAD OF TIME

- Agree on a place, time, and Saturday date for the art show with other families in the neighborhood. Give two or three weeks' notice.

- Make colorful signs about the event and post them on kitchen bulletin boards, fence posts, garage doors, and other places where they will attract attention.

- While all the children make art pieces for the show, the mothers or fathers can plan simple refreshments.

  NOTE: Any art can be entered: crayon drawings, paintings, clay sculpture, macramé, rock people, etc.

EARLY ON THE DAY OF THE EVENT

- Collect all entries at an early hour that has been announced in advance (e.g., 9:00 A.M.).

- Make sure each item is clearly marked with the name of the artist who created it.

- Separate entries into categories such as paintings, sculpture, drawings, etc.

- Set up displays, keeping categories together and arranging all entries so they may be clearly seen.

SHOW TIME

- Serve refreshments while parents and friends browse.

- Provide a cashier's table where art may be purchased for nickels, dimes, and quarters. Decide how money earned will be used. If it is to go to individual artists, have cashier keep track of items sold so money can be turned over to them when the show is over.

AFTERWARDS

- Make each artist responsible for picking up all unsold items and taking them home.

- Have a clean-up committee ready to put away tables and chairs, pick up trash, and see that leftover refreshments are properly taken care of.

SEASONS / SUMMER

BACKYARD CIRCUS

AHEAD OF TIME

- Pick a Saturday to have a circus, and choose a place to hold it.

- Invite the neighborhood children to plan circus acts.

- Invite parents, grandparents, and friends to come and be the audience.

- On the day of the circus, set up folding chairs and make small sacks of popcorn and a pitcher of cold lemonade.

YOUR CIRCUS MIGHT INCLUDE

- Clowns

- A trapeze artist doing tricks on a swing set

- A strong man lifting fake barbells or a cardboard box with "1000 lbs." written on it

- A pet parade

- An acrobat

- A dog show with dogs jumping through hoops, performing obedience tricks, etc.

- A balancing act on a balance beam or on a board placed over a sturdy child's pool filled with water

BACKYARD MINIATURE GOLF

For a special party or just for fun, set up a miniature "golf" course in the backyard. Instead of golf equipment, use croquet mallets and balls to play the course.

- Make flags to mark each hole out of small dowel sticks and construction paper or bright plastic. (A plastic disposable picnic tablecloth is an inexpensive and readily available resource.) Number the flags with broad-tipped felt pen or marker.

- Make a gravel or sand trap by putting down plastic sheeting and covering it with sand or small rocks from the driveway. (Pick up and replace later.)

- Use old boards and a brick, log, or cement block to make an incline to go up and over.

- Make a tunnel to go through from half of a hollow piece of log.

- Make an obstacle course from old paint cans set in rows.

- Use an old piece of guttering as a trough to go through. Drive small stakes on each side to hold it upright.

SEASONS / SUMMER

SEASONS / SUMMER

ONE PITCH SOFTBALL

This yard game is good when there are not enough players for full teams. It is a game without losers and scoring is kept only to measure length of play (as "we play until 20 runs are scored").

- Beginning with batter and pitcher, put a player at each position, using as many positions as you have players available.

- The pitcher throws one pitch (his best try) and the batter must try to hit it. If he misses, he is out. If he hits it, he runs.

- After this play all positions rotate. The pitcher becomes batter, batter (if he is out) goes to the outfield or third base, third baseman to second, second to first, and first becomes pitcher. If the original batter is on base, he tries to progress around the bases as new batters hit the ball. When he is "home" he takes his place in the rotation. As players successively fill the bases, there will be fewer defensive players and runners will find it easier to score. Enjoy!

- If there is a home run scored, that batter gets to bat again and no one rotates that round.

- When the score reaches the number originally agreed upon, the game is over.

THE SILENCE

Stillness is more audible than any sound, not tinny like so many sounds I hear these days.

The silence is full and rich, insistent . . . demanding that I listen and suggesting always that I'd be foolish not to. Only fools refuse the counsel of the wise, and this silence seems to know everything. It seems I've been a prodigal, traipsing along behind the band just like a thoughtless gypsy anywhere the living was easy, stealing morsels when I could have had the loaf.

Maybe it's the oaks and beeches. These oaks have housed a thousand generations of owls and jays, and have withstood abuse from countless woodpeckers and men. They've seen the fleet-footed native children tossing pebbles at their roots and chasing little fawns around between them. They've stood and heard the council casting lots for war or peace while fragrant pipe smoke wafted through their branches.

Perhaps it is the brook, whispering of its secret travels, nurturing the earth along its way, or maybe it's the earth, the pregnant fertile earth, pulling me like influential kin back to my moorings and my heritage.

The earth is calling me home to the simple and eternal things. It persistently calls me to reject the glitter of the transient and return to Father's house.

The silence—a voice asking one pointed and unavoidable question: will I return and inherit the earth? And here in the silence, the only sound to be heard is the whisper of my own answer.

SCHOOL DAYS

BACK-TO-SCHOOL SHOPPING SPREE

Make an "event" of shopping for back-to-school wardrobes. Spend some special time with each child alone.

- Go over last year's clothes; try everything on to see what still fits.

- Assess what may be handed down from an older brother or sister.

- Make a list of things needed to make the left-over wardrobe usable. List colors that are needed in accessories such as socks or belts.

- Make a realistic budget from the resources that are available. Explain the budget to the children. They will be more pleasant about "limitations" if they understand the budget and feel the parent is truly anxious to help.

- Plan a happy time looking for new things.

- Enjoy each other.

FIRST DAY OF SCHOOL

Make a special event of the first day of school. Try one or more of the following ideas, or create a tradition of your own:

- Wear one thing new.

- Take a picture to remember the day by.

- Go as a family to buy pencils, notebooks, and art supplies.

- Have a special "Celebrate Fall" supper of:

  chili
  vegetable sticks
  cheese slices
  assorted crackers
  homemade oatmeal cookies
  milk

CRAYON-LEAF TRANSFERS

MATERIALS NEEDED

White or light-colored construction paper
Crayons
Iron

- Collect strong leaves without holes or flaws. Green leaves are usually stronger and not so easily torn.

- With bright crayons, carefully color the back side of the leaves. You may color a leaf all one color, or shade in several colors.

- Lay the construction paper on an ironing board. Arrange the leaves on top with the colored side toward the paper.

- Iron the leaves with a medium to hot iron. You may iron through a sheet of waxed paper if you prefer not to iron directly onto the leaves.

- Remove the waxed paper and leaves. A crayoned print will be left on the construction paper.

- Decorate a wall, bulletin board, or bedroom door with these bright art pieces.

NOTE: This idea can be used to make personal stationery, note cards, or wrapping paper.

SEASONS / AUTUMN

WAXED PAPER

SEASONS / AUTUMN

STAINED GLASS LEAVES

MATERIALS NEEDED

Waxed paper
Construction paper
Glue
Scissors
Iron

- Collect brightly colored leaves of different sizes and shapes.

- Make two *identical* picture frames from two sheets of construction paper by cutting out the centers of the sheets. Cut a rectangle, square, oval, circle, or more ornate shape from the center of each sheet. The outer edge of the sheet can also be cut into whatever shape is desired for the frame.

- Cut a piece of waxed paper large enough so that, when it is folded double, it is larger than the cut-out center of the construction paper frame.

- Place one or two leaves inside the folded waxed paper.

- Iron with a medium to hot iron until waxed paper layers are sealed to each other around leaves.

- Place the sealed sheet containing the leaf or leaves between the two matching construction paper frames and glue the edges of the frames together.

- Tape "stained glass leaves" to windows or hang in front of windows from a thread.

NOTE: This activity can be adapted for spring wild flowers.

AUTUMN'S PROMISE OF SPRING

AHEAD OF TIME

Buy several dozen bulbs of various kinds like daffodil, tulip, hyacinth, crocus. Check with a local nursery, seed store, or county agent as to the best bulb-planting time in your area.

AT PLANTING TIME

- Wear warm jackets or sweatshirts, and protect your hands with garden gloves.

- Use shovels to dig up the area where bulbs are to be planted, turning over all the soil and breaking up clods of dirt; rake smooth.

NOTE: Let even small children help with shovels of their own.

- Take a moment to look at the bulbs and marvel at the unlikely miracle of life hidden within them.

- Plant bulbs so that the pointed side is up, about twice as deep as the height of bulb being planted. In very cold climates, plant the bulbs even deeper.

HINT: Check the package for predicted height of plant. Plant bulbs of tallest plants toward center of back of planting area, shorter plants toward outside or front. Leave 4 to 6 inches of space on all sides of each bulb.

- Cover entire plot with a layer of mulch, leaves, or peat moss.

- Celebrate the completed job with mugs of hot chocolate, cider, or herbal tea. Wait for a glorious spring!!

SEASONS / AUTUMN!

AUTUMN FAVORITES

Certain foods and beverages just seem to belong to special seasons. These two recipes surely say "Autumn's here!" (Of course, they're also good any time the weather's crisp.)

PUMPKIN PIE

Mix together:

> 1½ cups canned or freshly cooked and pureed pumpkin
> 2 eggs
> 1 cup sugar
> ½ tsp. each of salt, ginger, cinnamon, nutmeg
> 1 can condensed milk
>
> 2 8- or 9-inch unbaked pie shells

Fill shells and bake for 10 minutes at 425 degrees. Reduce heat to 350 degrees and bake for 35-40 minutes or until center of pie seems to be set.

HOT SPICED CIDER

- Fill a one-gallon percolator with cider.

- In percolator basket, place:

> 6 sticks cinnamon
> 8 whole cloves
> ½ lemon, cut into thin slices
> ¼ cup honey

- Perk as usual.

- Serve hot with a cinnamon stick or lemon slice in each cup.

SEASONS / AUTUMN

FIRST SNOW

- Make up a simple song or cheer to sing or yell together at the sight of the first snowflake.

- Decorate your home with paper snowflakes. Cut snowflakes from white paper and tape them on windows, doors, and blackboards. Make them by folding a piece of paper in half, then in half again three more times (four times altogether). Cut snips randomly from the corners and edges. Use your imagination, and no two will be alike. Unfold the paper and hang the snowflakes by black thread in doorways and from ceiling fixtures.

- Use the snowflake cutouts as stencils. Lay one or more stencil outlines on black paper and spray the cut-out areas with white or silver spray paint. The sheet may be displayed as a poster or you may want to cut out the spray-painted snowflakes and display them individually.

- Build "snowmen" and "snow forts" from marshmallows and toothpicks. Set them on a 9 x 11 piece of mirror and use the display for a table centerpiece.

- To make an unforgettable treat, try some snow ice cream from the following ingredients. Snow ice cream must be flavored to taste, so no proportions can be given. Just experiment until it is right. (It is unadvisable to make this recipe in areas of high pollution.)

SNOW ICE CREAM

Large pan or bowl full of clean, newly fallen snow

Cream

Vanilla

Granulated sugar

- Mix cream and vanilla together.

- Layer snow in a chilled bowl, sprinkling sugar on each layer.

- Fold flavored cream into snow. Don't let cream drain to the bottom, but keep tossing gently.

- Eat immediately, as soon as cream is frozen.

SEASONS / WINTER

SEASONS / WINTER

SNOWED-IN SUNDAY

If you live in an area where you are snowed in during the winter and you are unable to get out to church on Sunday morning, let the children plan a home worship service:

• Sing songs and hymns together using family talent (guitar, autoharp, piano, or other instruments) for accompaniment.

• Share prayer requests that affect and concern the whole family. (This might be a good time to talk about school problems or family concerns and needs.)

• Let each person tell the things for which he/she is thankful.

• Include a time of prayer. Let one child choose two or three persons to pray.

• Let the children plan and give the devotional thoughts. (Don't be surprised if their "sermon" is as long as the one at church!)

• Be sure no one leaves the "service" without being told that he/she is *loved*!

A WARM BEAR HUG

Heading for a bed that's been warmed by his/her own special teddy bear can make bedtime an event your child will look forward to. Here is an idea for assuring him/her a "warm bear hug" on any cool night.

- Choose washable fake fur material to make a teddy bear hot water bottle holder. Use a remnant or buy the yardage suggested for the pattern you will use.

- Select a simple teddy bear sewing pattern, making sure it can be adjusted to fit around the hot water bottle you plan to use.

- Modify the body length so that the bottle just fits the opening and the neck of the bottle fits up into the bear's head.

- Insert a zipper in the back seam.

- Double stitch all the seams that intersect the zipper. Also double stitch the seams around the zipper itself.

- Stuff the arms, legs, and head with old nylons or poly-fill material.

- Fill the bear-bottle with hot water while the child is getting ready for bed, and tuck the cuddly animal between the sheets. Make sure it is not too hot for the child to touch.

- The bear will retain heat for several hours.

SEASONS / WINTER

TAFFY PULL

This special winter memory-maker is fun for all ages. Try it with a bunch of teenagers, two or three whole families, or three or four couples.

Here are some rules and ahead-of-time warnings:

- If you don't boil molasses long enough, it won't harden like it should as it is worked. (In this case, it will end up all over your hands, which is fun, too. Just eat it off!)

- Boiled down syrup is unmercifully hot! It quickly and severely burns anything it touches, so advise participants before starting that there will be no horsing around while syrup is being poured!

- If the taffy is to turn out white instead of sickly gray, hands that pull it must be very clean.

OLD FASHIONED MOLASSES TAFFY

⅔ cup molasses
⅓ cup light corn syrup
1½ cups firmly packed brown sugar
1½ Tbsp. vinegar
½ cup water
¼ tsp. salt
•
⅛ tsp. soda
¼ cup butter

Combine molasses, syrup, brown sugar, vinegar, water, and salt in large, heavy saucepan, stirring until sugar dissolves over low heat. Cook, stirring occasionally, until mixture reaches 265 degrees on candy thermometer. Remove from heat and stir in soda and butter. Pour into buttered large shallow pan and let cool until it can be handled—about 15 minutes. Turn edges in to center as it cools. Butter your fingertips; then cut off pieces of candy and pull and twist until candy changes color, to bronze. Twist in shapes or cut into 1-inch pieces with scissors dipped in cold water. Wrap in plastic paper. Makes 150 pieces.

NOTE FROM GLORIA: My grandma used to spread peanut butter on a flat strip of pulled taffy, roll peanut butter inside, seal edges, then snip off pieces with the scissors. These she wrapped in little pieces of waxed paper and twisted the ends to seal. I can just see her doing it!

WINTER GARDEN

While nothing is growing outside, start a garden inside. You can grow the following vegetables in your kitchen window:

• Beans

Fill sections of an egg carton or small dixie cups with potting soil. Soak bean seeds or dried beans that have been purchased for cooking (navy beans, pinto beans, butter beans, etc.) in water overnight. Push two beans into the soil in each cup until they are just below the surface; then cover them. Water each day.

• Carrots

Cut off the tops of several carrots, leaving about one inch of carrot attached to top. Place carrot tops in a saucer or pie pan and add enough water to keep the bottom of each piece in water. Do not allow them to dry out. Before long, roots will form and new tops will grow.

• Sweet potatoes

Cut sweet potatoes in the same way as carrots, and use the same method to grow green tops. Toothpicks can be inserted into vegetable pieces and used to support them from the rim of a small glass. Keep enough water in the glass that the bottom of the vegetable cutting stays submerged.

• Alfalfa sprouts or bean sprouts

Fold several thicknesses of paper towel and place in the bottom of a flat bowl or large saucer. Soak the towel with water and sprinkle alfalfa seeds or beans on the soaked towels. Keep towels wet. In a few days the seeds will sprout and can be used in salads or on sandwiches. Sprouts can also be grown in a fruit jar. Put just enough water in the jar to partially cover the seeds. Put on the jar lid. As the water inside the jar evaporates, the air will become very humid, eventually condensing on the underside of the lid and "raining" down again on the seeds. The seeds will sprout within a few days, and a "garden" will grow inside your jar.

SEASONS / WINTER

BIRDSEED PRETZELS

Birdseed Pretzels are sure to draw a winter crowd of feathered guests. Explain to your children how difficult it is for birds to find enough to eat at this time of year and how much they can help by providing attractive food for them. To prepare Birdseed Pretzels:

- Cut a 12-inch piece of waxed paper and lay it flat on a protected surface. The corners may have to be taped down so the paper doesn't curl while the pretzels are being made.

- Squirt fairly wide lines (about ¼ inch) of Elmer's Glue on the waxed paper to form a pretzel-like design in which all lines meet.

- Sprinkle bird seed or sunflower seeds to cover all the glue.

- Allow to dry overnight.

- Turn designs upside down on a flat surface and *carefully* peel away the waxed paper.

- Hang on limbs or fences with thread.

ANYTIME ACTIVITIES

THE FIRST TO SHARE

Celebrate the arrival of nature's first fruits by sharing as a family:

- The first lettuce from the garden.

- The first rose bud. Place it in a prominent place and enjoy its beauty together.

- The first apple from the tree. Divide it and make every bite count!

- The first cider. Go as a family to buy it. Make a tradition of it by always serving it some special way: with popcorn, hot with cinnamon sticks and honey, or straight from the jug.

- The first pumpkin pie. Make a tradition of inviting the same guest(s) to share it—a grandparent, friend, neighbor, or other relative.

DRAWING CONTEST

Plan a time for the family to be creative together. Drawing is a good outlet, and—who knows? —maybe you will find you have an artist in the family!

- Ask everyone in the family to draw a picture of what he/she thinks the present season would look like if it were a person. This can be done at the beginning of each new season. For example, ask, "If Spring were a person, what would he/she look like?"

- Have each person use color and detail to show what that season's personality and style seems to be.

- Sit in a circle and share the drawings with each other.

- Have each person explain why he/she pictures the season as he/she did.

- Thank God together for the uniqueness of each season.

POP SONGS

- You will need eight empty pop bottles, all the same size.

- Fill each one with a different level of water. (The more water, the higher the pitch that will sound when the bottle is struck.)

- Adjust the amounts of water in each bottle until you have the right amount to play the notes of a musical scale. Tap each bottle with a metal spoon to check its pitch.

- Let each family member have a turn playing a familiar melody or creating a new one.

SEASONS / ANY TIME OF YEAR

PARTY PUNCHBOARD

A punchboard is fun to use as a crazy game of chance at a party or other group gathering, or just for the family for after-supper fun. Traditional commercial punchboards are ½" to ¾" thick boards in which holes have been made at regular intervals and then filled with rolled-up slips of paper containing printed messages. The holes are then covered over with paper. The person buying a turn at the punchboard then punches through the paper covering the hole he selects and extracts the printed message from it. A home version of the game can easily be made from inexpensive materials readily available in most households. You will need:

> an empty milk carton or a small, shallow jewelry box
> several sheets of plain paper
> several drinking straws, cut into ½" lengths, or a supply of tiny rubber bands of the type worn with dental braces

- Cut off the milk carton about 1 inch above the bottom; discard the top. Use the bottom portion as a shallow tray, or use the bottom or the lid of the jewelry box. This tray will hold the paper messages for the game.

- Cut the sheets of paper into strips approximately 1" wide and write a fun instruction on each strip. (See ideas below, but be prepared to use your imagination for the number of messages that you will need for filling the tray.)

- Roll each strip tightly and stuff it into a section of paper straw tubing or secure it with a tiny rubber band.

- Stand the rolls on end in the tray or box. Make enough rolls to fill the tray completely.

- Play the game by having each person in turn poke a sharpened pencil into the center of a message-tube and pull it out. The player must then follow whatever instructions the message gives.

SAMPLE MESSAGES:

> Try to touch your elbow with your tongue.
> Trade socks with another person.
> Pick up a Lifesaver on a toothpick held in your teeth and carry it across the room.
> Teach the others a new aerobic exercise.
> Teach the others a cheer you learned in school.
> Tell what three books you would take to a desert island.
> Tell one thing you like about each person present.
> Run outside, touch your toes three times without bending your knees, and then skip back to the group.
> Bark like a small, nervous dog.

MAKING MEMORIES IN SPECIAL PLACES

SPECIAL PLACES / VACATIONS

GETTING READY FOR VACATION

VACATION TIME/ ADVENTURE TIME

Make vacation time an adventure for the whole family. Here are some ideas for family discussion:

Take a cruise
Stay on a working farm
Take a backpacking expedition
Go white-water rafting
Stay at a real working western guest ranch
Participate in a cattle drive
Go mountaineering
Take a hiking vacation in the great northwest
Stay on an island
Learn to snorkel, ski, soar in a balloon, canoe, sail
Visit a country inn

For addresses, prices, and descriptions of ways and places to go on vacations like these, request a catalog or send for these books from The Berkshire Traveller Travel Shelf:

Adventure Travel
Country Inns and Back Roads
Farm, Ranch, Country Vacations

Berkshire Traveller Press
Stockbridge, MA 01262

DRAW A VACATION

Let the entire family help decide what kind of vacation to take this year.

- Obtain enough computer paper, brown wrapping paper, or shelf paper for the whole family to draw a wall mural. Choose a place to display it when it is finished; then measure off the amount of paper to fit the space that is available.

- After dinner, let each member of the family draw a favorite vacation or trip on his or her section of the mural. Use crayons, marker pens, or paints.

- Discuss what everyone would like to do *this* year.

- Hang the finished product in the place that has been chosen for it. Seeing and talking about each person's ideas may help the family decide on a vacation that will be more fun for everyone.

VACATION SURVIVAL BAG

Pack a special duffel or tote bag with vacation craft supplies. Some "musts" are:

  bag of plaster of Paris
  white glue
  string, yarn, or old shoestrings
  jackknife
  box of crayons
  box of colored chalk
  drawing paper
  pipe cleaners or chenille craft wires
  Scotch tape
  play dough (this is handy for making plaster of Paris molds)
  empty notebook for writing poems, memories and vacation notes
  small plant press

TRAVEL FUN

GOURMET TRAVELER

- Collect menus of all the restaurants enjoyed by the family while on the trip.

- Arrange them in an attractive grouping on a den or in a hallway. (Decorators often use this idea.)

- Other objects can be added to form an interesting display.

- Be creative!

MAP MATTERS

- On a traveling vacation, take along a map of the area you are going to visit.

- Have the children trace the route with a marking pen as you travel.

- Look on the map at what lies north, south, east, and west of your route. Talk about the climate, terrain, agriculture, industry of the area, and interesting sights you see out the window of your car, plane, train, or bus.

GAMES IN THE CAR

- Draw 2-inch squares on 4 x 6 cards. Before leaving on the trip, list in each square an object which you may see on your journey such as a barn, horse, etc. Later, when you see the object listed on your card, call it out and mark it off. The first to finish his card is the winner.

- While the driver watches the odometer, each family member tries to guess when he or she thinks the car has gone one or five or ten miles. The one who is closest wins a point.

- The "Alphabet Game" is played with letters on road signs and businesses. The first person who gets through the alphabet wins. The winner gets to choose the restaurant for dinner.

- As a family project during a long journey, attempt to locate and record on paper at least one license plate number from all fifty states and the District of Columbia. (Some resort centers have dozens of cars from out of state.)

VACATION MEMENTOES

TREASURE TRIP

- Collect natural treasures on your trip such as sea shells, starfish, sand dollars, flowers, leaves, rocks, seed pods, bird nests, pine cones, cocoons, pieces of wood.

- After the trip is over, display your collection on a table or fireplace mantel, or glue them in an interesting design on heavy poster board.

- Discuss when, where and how the treasures were found and in what locations, etc.

MEMORY COLLAGE

- Take along a bottle of white glue on your trip.

- Collect pieces of bark, driftwood, or flat rock to use as a base for your collage.

- Collect small objects from each picnic site, hike, boat trip, mountain climb, etc.

- Spend one evening (or rainy day) toward the end of the trip arranging the memory objects and gluing them to the base.

- On the back, write the place and date of your vacation. Attach a gummed hanger or wire to the back for hanging.

VACATION ANNUAL

- Buy a durable empty book at an art shop, novelty shop, or bookstore.

- Label the front cover "Vacation Book."

- Take it on each vacation and label a fresh section for each vacation, for example: "Grand Canyon, June 1979" or "Big Sur, June 1981."

- Draw pictures to depict the sorts of things you did on the trip.

- Have each person in the family, any guests, and anyone you meet and get to know, write in the book. Share thoughts, special moments, funny incidents, poetry, etc. Be sure to have each person sign his/her name. Have the children include their ages.

- Save the book for the next vacation and begin a new section.

Reading over old entries can bring back lovely memories as well as bring a good laugh: "Look how Tommy wrote when he was three!" "Remember, Grandma went with us on that trip."

LATE SUMMER VACATION
BEAVER ISLAND, MICHIGAN

Curtain call to summer . . .

Seems as though the action should only just be starting.
School begins this week, but vacation holds us a few days longer for
       its own education.
Pines against the blue, blue sky;
White sails slithering between resting white gulls;
Quaint little buildings clustered along the northeast cove,
    huddled together the better to withstand the tides of
          both the water and the world—
    simple, practical structures, preserved and cared for but without
       trim and frills,
    painted white, mostly, to protect against wind and weather.

I will my mind's eye to memorize, imprint indelibly,
    images of our treasured time together.
Benjy and Amy, racing down the dunes,
    squealing and scooting on their bottoms to the water's edge;
Suzanne, sitting apart, piling sand,
    thinking, changing, turning, reluctant to let go of childhood.
What moments will they remember?

Ferry ride adventure in a simple, awkward tub of a boat,
    blunt, high, like Noah's ark.
        (We could be animals, hanging out from little corners of the
        deck, stormy water tossing us around like marbles in a cup,
        with not even a raven we can send to reconnoiter.)
Journey by a narrow road through the virgin timber
    to roast hot dogs beside a hidden lake.
Outrageous liquid crimson moon rising out of a satin sea,
    fresh from the moon-vat,
    dripping until suspended and attached to the black sandpaper sky.

Easy alliance of sausage and sunrise,
    mellowed by the aroma of hot coffee and comfortable relationships,
    shared in cottages warmed by itinerant children.
Bicycle rides to the village,
    past greedy gulls' feeding ground littered with man's castaways—
    mutilated T-bones, sardines, chicken bones, bread crusts
    (my apple coffeecake, too, toll for crossing to their side of the island)
    —but few shells, except for clams
        (only experts find good ones).
Icy little stream, numbing bare feet;
    beside its banks rocks, flat, shaved,
    perfect for skipping two, three, four times with practice.
        ("Everybody throw when I say three!
        One, two, three!")
Old abandoned car, almost hidden by weeds and scrub,
    wooden-spoked wheels and running board outlasting metal body.
Moss, a hundred kinds, plush, extravagant;
Indian peacepipes, smoked silently, unseen and uncensured;
Monarchs and bank swallows, flitting between my thoughts,
    smell of cedar overpowering my consciousness.
Loons, gulls, nightingales, human voices are stilled by insistent
         silence
    while the setting sun plays out its drama on this last night.

Too soon, the departing ferry's sharp announcement breaks the spell,
    and reminds of summer's end.
Leaving this quaint, quiet place, I rejoice
    that its peace and solitude are portable;
    that as we walk crowded streets,
          noisy school corridors,
          busy office building hallways,
          familiar stairways in our own bustling house,
    the tranquility given to our souls may remain.

SOIL DIARY

- Take small clean baby food jars. (If you don't have a baby, ask someone who does to save some jars for you.)

- On each vacation or out-of-state family outing, fill a jar with the soil from the place you visit.

- Label the sample with the date and place.

NOTE: Plastic wrap under the lid will prevent moisture from rusting the lid.

- Display the collection on a shelf or mantel at home or in a summer cottage.

SUGGESTION: Find out what is grown in the soil in each of the following areas and what conditions produced its color and texture.

    Red Georgia clay
    Hawaiian black volcanic sand
    Wisconsin loam
    Michigan brown sand from Lake Huron
    White sand from Florida
    Orange (iron) soil from Copper Harbor, Michigan
    Volcanic dust (from Mt. St. Helens)
    Salt from Utah

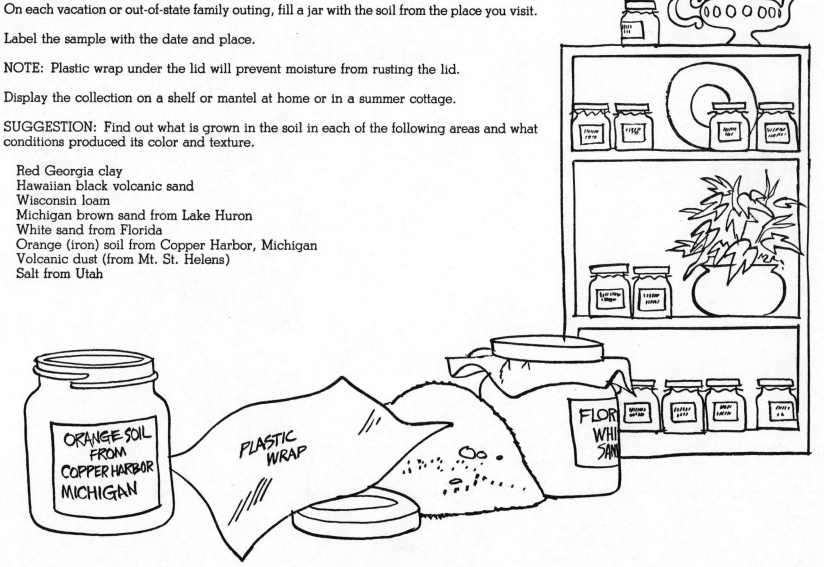

ORANGE SOIL FROM COPPER HARBOR MICHIGAN

PLASTIC WRAP

FLOR WHI SAN

SPECIAL PLACES / VACATIONS

SPECIAL PLACES / VACATIONS

AN UNVACATION

When you are unable to take a vacation because of financial strain, time limitations, or other reason, here are some ideas that can be fun, interesting, and even educational:

• Attend a court session.

• Go to a museum.

• Visit the factories or large businesses in your area. Some may have regular tours.

• Go to an art gallery.

• Check out a book at the library to be read aloud to the whole family.

• Go to the park.

• Go to the beach.

• Attend a city council meeting.

• Watch for bargain sales at material stores and make back-to-school wardrobes. (This is a good time for daughters to learn how to sew.)

• Visit another church that has a different kind of worship service from your own church.

FOREST FOSSILS

MATERIALS NEEDED

Plaster of Paris
Plant press or two flat pieces of wood and a rock
Plastic-coated paper plate or Styrofoam plate

- Collect different kinds of leaves, blossoms, seeds, pods, and insects.

- Press the leaves and blossoms overnight in a plant press or between two pieces of wood weighted with a rock. A huge book will work, too. Be sure to put a layer of paper towel on each side of the leaves to keep moisture from damaging the pages of the book. This removes natural moisture from the leaves, which otherwise will curl when placed in the plaster of Paris or will fail to adhere to it permanently, if that is desired.

- Mix a small portion of plaster of Paris with enough water to make a mixture about the consistency of cake batter. Pour into a paper plate.

- Before the plaster hardens, press the specimens into the plaster until a definite imprint is made; then remove. You may remove the specimens or leave them imbedded in plaster.

- As the plaster hardens, it will feel warm. After it cools completely and has set firmly, gently remove it from the plate. If you wish to hang your forest fossils, attach a large gummed hanger to the reverse side.

SPECIAL PLACES / WOODS

REMINDERS OF THE WOODS

WOODLAND RUBBINGS

MATERIALS NEEDED

Thin drawing or typing paper
Crayons or chalk

The woods are full of lovely textures. Find an interesting surface such as the back side of a leaf, the bark of a tree, a fossil rock, the rough cap of an acorn, the knobby surface of a hedge-apple, Osage orange, etc.

- Make a "rubbing" by placing paper over the textured surface and rubbing back and forth carefully with crayon or chalk. Like magic, the texture will be recorded on your paper.

- Label the texture, if you like, then display your woodland rubbing on the cabin door or paste it in your vacation scrapbook.

WOODLAND MOBILE

Collect small specimens such as:

  bark
  algae or lichens
  dried weed pods
  large seeds
  pine cones
  pebbles from a brook-bed

When you get back to camp or home, tie woodland treasures to a clothes hanger with differing lengths of string, thread or yarn. Hang it indoors or in a sheltered spot outdoors.

MACARONI JEWELS

MATERIALS NEEDED

Macaroni of different sizes
String, yarn, or shoestrings

Some rainy evening in camp, make jewelry by stringing all kinds of macaroni (any kind with a large hole) onto string or shoestrings.

HINT: Yarn can be made easy to thread by wrapping a piece of Scotch tape around one end or by dipping the end of the yarn in melted wax.

SPECIAL PLACES / WOODS

DIONIS BEACH

This last night of our vacation we had a wiener roast on the Dionis Beach. Then we searched the water for little creatures, and found dozens of hermit crabs and other kinds of sea life. This beach is certainly our favorite—so quiet, so secretive and promising, so romantic. Benjy's, Amy's and Suzanne's profiles between the pink horizon and the quiet sea are frozen in my mind as if someone had stopped a movie projector to take a closer look at one frame—this frame—this moment. Benjy, so innocent on the outer edge of childhood—all freckled and wind-blown with his sun-bleached hair and dancing eyes, his sturdy little body and wide, strong hands. Amy, so straight and tall with her first "real hairdo"—excited, bubbling, expectant, and always optimistic, always making peace and making do with whatever circumstances or people she has to work with. Suzanne, poised on the path to womanhood, yet wise enough to keep her childhood's wide-eyed wonder and excitement over simple things—protective, inventive and loyal with an eye for art and beauty; self-sufficient, yet needing to be loved and touched and protected, too.

I see their faces there between the sea and sky. Barely children they are, yet hardly mature. I stand on tiptoe and try to hold this moment in my mind, for this visit to our precious island will be like no other. We've celebrated the happy days of childhood here on these beaches and watched the little footprints in the sand. Now we make this island our welcome mat for grown-up days. If I look closely down this beach I can see the prints of tiny toddler feet grow bigger as they run along until they end right here in front of me, long and slim and almost the size of mine. Growing feet. Running feet. Feet I've held in my hand and counted "piggies" on. Feet I've scrubbed the mud and sand and grass stain from. Feet I've tied sneakers on and guided into stiff, new Sunday shoes. Feet I've taught to pedal bikes and to roller skate. Feet I've taught to paddle when they swim and hold "just so" in stirrups when riding horses, with toes pointed in and heels out. Feet that have learned to go where I couldn't follow . . . up tall trees, down school hallways, on dates. I've watched those feet take first steps, toddle, walk, skip, balance, kick footballs, run bases, march in parades, and dance pirouettes. And at every stage I've watched them leave the current footwear behind to run barefoot and free down these beloved beaches.

FOOTPRINTS IN TIME

As your children grow, you may often wish you could "hang onto them" just the way they are at that moment. Permanent "footprints" made from year to year serve to fill that yearning and at the same time make an interesting record of each child's growth.

- Pack a plastic bag full of plaster of Paris in your suitcase.

- At the beach, mix the plaster and the required amount of water (fresh water—salt water will not set).

- Have each child make a clear, deep footprint in damp sand.

- Pour the print full of plaster.

- Let the plaster stand until it is semi-soft. Then insert a bent hair pin into the plaster for a hanger.

- When the plaster cast is cool and hard, dig away the sand and remove the "footprint."

- On the back of each footprint, write the person's name, age, and the place where the footprint was made.

- Repeat each year, and keep a collection on a special wall or in each child's room.

SPECIAL PLACES / WATER'S EDGE

SAND CASTLES

It is great fun for the whole family to work together to build a sand kingdom, using wet sand and various molds such as sand buckets, empty coffee cans, cottage cheese and yogurt cartons, or clean soup cans.

Try a more fantastic sculpture by building close enough to the ocean to dig a small pit that fills up with water. Now, take dripping wet handfuls of sand from the pit and drizzle them in mounds away from the pit. As soon as the drippings hit the ground they will drain, leaving beautiful sculptured peaks. These castles can have dozens of pencil thin towers and spires.

Now add sticks and bits of Kleenex for flags, use fingers to drill tunnels, and make moats to protect your kingdom.

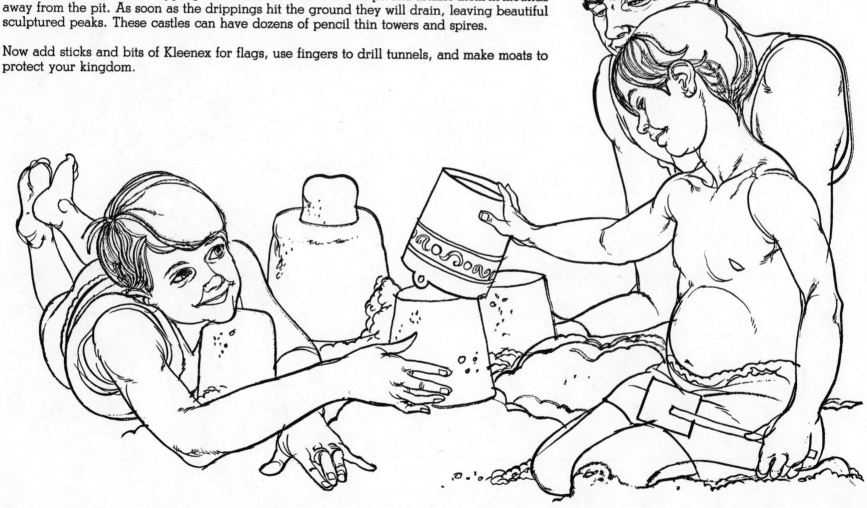

CLAMBAKE

AHEAD OF TIME

Choose a beach location for your clambake and check for permission to build a fire there. Gather the supplies and cooking utensils you will need.

MATERIALS NEEDED

A clam boiler or large enameled pot with lid
A pailful of fresh water
Lots of seaweed
One baking potato for each person (wrap potatoes in foil)
One or two pieces of uncooked chicken, per person, each piece wrapped in cheesecloth
One lobster for each person
One ear of corn per person. Leave corn in husks, then wrap in foil
Plenty of steamer clams
Melted butter

AT THE BEACH

- Dig a small pit, and lay a charcoal and wood fire.

- Dig clams; then scrub them with a brush and soak them in a pail of fresh water for an hour or more.

- Rinse the seaweed several times in clean water; then soak for an hour to get rid of sand.

- Line bottom of clam pot with a 4-inch layer of seaweed and add one quart of fresh water.

- Put pot over hot fire until water boils. Then add wrapped potatoes and more seaweed. Cover with lid and cook for fifteen minutes on lower fire.

- Add chicken and more clean seaweed. Cover and wait fifteen more minutes.

- Add lobsters and more seaweed. Cover again and cook five more minutes before adding corn. Cook ten minutes more.

- Add clams now and steam until clams pop open (about ten minutes). All the cooking will take about an hour. Melted butter can be served in clam shells.

- Be sure to have lots of paper napkins handy because this meal will be messy, but delicious and great fun!

SPECIAL PLACES / WATER'S EDGE

SEASIDE SOUVENIRS

SEA CHIMES

MATERIALS NEEDED

A small inexpensive wicker basket or wicker hot pad
String
Lots of shells that have holes through them

- Tie a string to exact center of hot pad or basket bottom, knotting the string securely so it will not pull through when the chimes are hung. At the free end of the string, make a loop for hanging the chimes.

- String shells in several lengths of string, tying knots to leave small spaces between the shells.

- Tie the strands of shells around the rim of the basket or hot pad.

- Hang the sea chimes in an open place, for example, from a porch ceiling or under a deck.

SEA JEWELRY

- Gather together an assortment of inexpensive baubles from the variety store such as:

  plastic hair combs
  wide plastic rings
  plain wide plastic bracelets

- You will also need:

  white glue
  tiny colorful shells
  tweezers

- Make tiny dots of white glue on the surface you'd like to decorate.

- With tweezers, place a tiny shell on each drop of glue. Continue until the comb, bracelet, or ring is beautifully decorated with seashore "jewels."

SEASIDE COLLAGE

To make this collage you will need to remember to bring some white glue or clear cement from home.

- Collect from your beachcombing walks:

    a large flat piece of driftwood
    other small bits of driftwood
    pretty shells
    bits of dry seaweed, special pebbles, seagull feathers, or anything else you find of interest
    things that help you remember good times: ticket stubs, old keys, bottle caps, corner torn from a trail map, etc.

- Use the flat driftwood as a base.

- Glue the smaller items to the driftwood in any arrangement you think is artistic.

- Tack a picture hanger to the back and display your collage on a wall at home, or use the collage as a special centerpiece for the table.

PRIZE PRINTS

To make Prize Prints, you will need to take along with you to the beach some India ink or tempera paint and a few squares of white muslin.

- Take your prize fish or favorite sea creature to a sandy place on the bank, *after* you have rinsed it off well.

- Dry it or let it dry.

- Paint one side of the fish with India ink or tempera paint.

- Cover the inked side of the fish with a piece of clean muslin. Gently press the cloth against the fish and rub the cloth with your hand, being careful not to scoot the cloth as you do so.

- Carefully lift the cloth.

- Wash the fish again; then go ahead and clean it up to cook for supper.

- Take the life-size print of your prize catch or find home with you and mount the print on a piece of plywood or Masonite.

DESERT TREASURES

DESERT SHADOW BOX

MATERIALS NEEDED

A sturdy box (gift box or sawed-off shoe box)
Poster board or heavy construction paper
Glue
Desert finds such as small stones, bones, dried
  cactus, seed pods, feathers, plaster castings
  of small animal footprints, etc.

- Make partitions in the box with strips of poster board the same width as the depth of the box.

- Cut the strips enough longer to allow you to bend each end to make a tab to be glued to box. "Windows" in your box may be symmetrical, or you may prefer to make them random sizes.

- If you like, spray paint the box before going on to the next step.

- Glue tiny treasures in each window, taking care to balance sizes and shapes artistically.

- When you get home, stand the box on end. Place a desert book and a candle alongside to make a lovely centerpiece or table display.

DESERT TREASURE STORAGE BOX

MATERIALS NEEDED

An egg carton
Pieces of contact paper or colorful stickers

Decorate the lid of an egg carton with desert designs, letters, or desert flowers cut from contact paper or with colorful stickers. Fill the carton with special desert finds.

DESERT IN A JAR

MATERIALS NEEDED

A clean, wide-mouthed half gallon or gallon
  pickle jar with holes in the lid
Sand
Small desert rocks or dried broken bits of dead
  cactus
Small live cactus plants (do not take cacti from
  the desert; buy them in desert stores)

• Pour about two inches of sand in the bottom
  of a clean jar. Plant cactus plants, being
  careful not to get prickles in your fingers.
  (Cotton garden gloves might make the job
  more pleasant.)

• Place a few colorful rocks or broken bits of
  dead cacti around the plants.

• Add a small amount of water, just enough to
  dampen the sand.

• Place the lid on the jar and put your desert
  garden in a sunny window.

SPECIAL PLACES / DESERT

SAND LAYERING

- Bring home a bag of sand from your vacation to do sand layering. You will need:

    sand
    a clear jar with lid (tall thin olive jars, short fat pimento jars, jelly jars, pickle jars, etc.)
    plastic cups (not Styrofoam)
    paper towels
    powdered fabric dyes or food coloring

- Set out as many plastic cups as you want colors of sand, and fill each cup half full of sand.

- In another cup, mix water and as much dye powder or drops of food coloring as it takes to make the color you want. Remember the dyed sand will be lighter than the colored water, so go a shade or two darker.

- Pour colored water into the cup of sand and stir with a plastic spoon.

- Rinse the water cup before repeating the coloring process with each new color of sand.

- When all the cups of sand have dye in them, let them stand at least fifteen minutes.

- Carefully drain the water off of the sand. (It's better to do this outside so that no grains of sand will go down the drain.)

- Cover a worktable or countertop with waxed paper; then lay out four sheets of paper towel (four thicknesses) for each color of sand. Spoon the sand onto paper towels, spread it out a bit, and let it dry. Keep colors separate.

- After the sand is dry, carefully begin to spoon it into dry jars in beautiful layers. You can make "mountains" and "valleys" by mounding sand of one color against the side of the jar, filling in the valleys with another color.

NOTE: This activity can also be enjoyed after a "water's edge" vacation.

SAND PAINTINGS

MATERIALS NEEDED

Brightly colored chalk
Sand samples
Baby food jars or empty 35mm film containers
White glue
Manila paper or poster board

- Collect sand samples of different textures.

- Crush some brightly colored chalk and mix with sand to create desired colors.

- "Paint" your picture with glue, one item at a time.

- Then sprinkle colored sand on the glue. Tip picture gently to remove excess sand. Collect this sand on another piece of paper; then return unused colored sand to container.

- Keep adding glue and colored sand until your painting is finished.

HINT: If you first "paint" the background such as sky, sea, mountains, fields, and let this part dry for a few hours, you can add more detail (buds, trees, flowers, boats), even on top of the dried background.

SPECIAL PLACES / DESERT

SPECIAL PLACES / MOUNTAINS

ALTITUDE FOLIAGE DIARY

AHEAD OF TIME

Pack in your backpack some sort of book which can double as devotional and a press for this project.

- At each altitude, collect samples of foliage. Place between book pages to preserve. Include with each sample a slip of paper identifying it by number according to the order in which it was collected.

- In a diary, use corresponding numbers to describe the terrain of the elevation at which each sample was found.

- When you return to camp or home, mount each sample on a separate sheet of art paper or page of a scrapbook, and record any comments about what you experienced the day the sample was found and a description of the terrain or view.

- Protect the pages with a cover page on which you write your name, date, mountain area climbed, and state; or, glue a title page to the scrapbook that you have used.

- Keep it where your family can look through it often to recall happy memories.

MOVING ALERT

MOVING TO A NEW HOME

- Discuss with young children the things in the house that will be moved. Be sure they are assured that their beds, trucks, favorite stuffed animals, records, etc., will go along.

  NOTE: This is *not* a good time to sort out old toys, games, tennis shoes, etc. Neither should you change from crib to bed, do away with bedtime blanket or pacifier, or drastically change feeding habits.

- See that the whole family, including young children, is involved in the moving process. Even young children can neatly stack wash cloths, towels, or dish towels into a box or fill a container with stuffed toys, paper products, canned goods, utensils or lids, plastic ware or books.

- When you arrive at the new place, assemble the children's rooms first and unpack their favorite things. Be sure the children are present for this even if they have to be left with a neighbor or grandparent while the heavy work is done.

SPECIAL PLACES / NEW HOME

MUSICAL PACKAGES

To make the chore of packing—or unpacking—go faster, try playing this game while the family works together.

- Choose one person to be "it."

- The person who is "it" hums a tune for the others to guess.

- When someone else recognizes the song, he/she shouts "I know the words!" and then proves it by singing back the phrase with the words.

- That person then gets to hum a favorite tune.

A STARRY WELCOME

BEFORE LEAVING YOUR PRESENT HOME

- Spend time as a family outside at night.

- Look at the stars; find the Milky Way, the Big Dipper, the Little Dipper.

- Watch the moon rise, and notice its path and size. Is it full? Quarter?

- Find the North Star, Orion, Cassiopeia.

AFTER ARRIVING AT YOUR NEW HOME

- Leave all the boxes and unpacking for a few minutes each night during the first week.

- Sit quietly as a family in your new yard, on the porch or balcony, or rooftop, if it is safe for everyone.

- Try to find each familiar constellation.

- Talk about the comfort you find in knowing the same sky and heavenly lights are there to welcome you.

- Thank God together for the earth, the sky, and the gift of having each other no matter where you may go.

(If you've moved to another continent, you may find that the summer sky back home is the winter sky of your new home; or the placement of stars may be different.)

NOTE: A whole-family hug is the best warmth on a chilly evening!

GET ACQUAINTED TREASURE HUNT

- While everyone is busy unloading, hide small surprises or treats around the nooks and crannies of the new house and yard.

- Choose a time when everyone needs a break.

- Give each child a small sack, and send the family out to find the treasures.

- When everyone returns, share the treats and a cool glass of iced tea or lemonade or a cup of hot chocolate, depending on the time of year.

MAKING MEMORIES WITH SPECIAL PEOPLE

FAMILY ROOTS

Most children have very little knowledge of their grandparents' earlier years, yet this background offers one of the richest sources of tradition and identity within a family. Children love to listen to the folklore and the stories that grandparents spin so well, and intergenerational discussions reward everyone with meaningful moments of family history, fun, and love. To give your children this important historical perspective and family bonding:

- Plan a visit to each set of grandparents, prearranging that the theme of the visit will be to have the grandparents share their reminiscences of earlier years and their information about family background.

- Gather the whole family group together after the evening meal (on as many evenings as the length of the visit permits) for a time of listening as the older generation talks. If the visit takes place during cold weather and a fireplace is available, build a fire in the fireplace for the family to gather around.

- A tape recorder or video recorder may be used, with the grandparents' permission, to record these priceless memories.

SPECIAL THINGS FOR GRANDPARENTS TO DO WITH GRANDCHILDREN

- Make it a part of every visit to tell your grandchildren (other children, too) some of the things you remember when you were their age that are no longer a part of their lives today. Talk about how things were done, tools and equipment used, various kinds of transportation, family customs and activities, school life, dating and courtship, how you met and married.

- Share a meal each week with your grandchildren (Saturday breakfast, Sunday dinner, Tuesday after-school snack). Make it always the same. Kids love traditions and habits!

- Keep a supply of storybooks. Make it a part of every visit to read a story together with your grandchildren. You do the reading when they're very small. As they learn to read, you can share the reading aloud.

- While they're still small enough to sit on your lap, read the Sunday comics aloud to your grandchildren.

- Let small children name animals while you respond by mimicking the sound that animal makes. Switch roles and let the child make the sounds while you name the animal. Use great drama and animation.

- Take older children (ages 7–15) on bird-watching hikes. Take binoculars and a good bird resource book.

- Take your grandchildren on a nature hike. Take binoculars if you are in an area where wildlife may be seen, and resource books that contain helpful information about what you expect to see. Collect, press, and mount wildflowers in a scrapbook.

- Bird, animal, tree, and wildflower resource books may be ordered from the National Wildlife Federation. For information, write to the Federation at: 1412 Sixteenth Street N.W., Washington, D.C. 20036.

GRANDPARENTS / GRANDCHILDREN

gloria gloria gloria gloria gloria gloria gloria gloria gloria gloria gloria gloria

TO BE A MAN

My little nephew was playing on the floor with his trucks one fine spring morning. His grandma was standing at the sink washing a dishpanful of tender, fresh leaf lettuce; some of the first to be harvested in town.

"What are you going to be when you grow up?" his grandma asked.

David crawled across the floor, pushing his toy tractor and making motor noises with his mouth.

"Would you like working in a big factory or having an office of your own? Are you going to be a teacher? Or maybe a fireman or a policeman?"

David crawled closer to the back screen door, which was open to the pungent fragrance of freshly turned soil. He ran his little tractor up the door, then stopped, looking out at his grandfather plowing the warm earth with the garden tractor.

"Nope," he finally said, "I just wanna be a man, like my grandpa!"

Lord, our world is so in need of heroes. Give us fewer "professionals" and more men who stand tall in integrity and gentle strength and godliness. Thank you that a real one lives at our house. Amen.

gloria gloria gloria gloria gloria gloria gloria gloria gloria gloria gloria gloria gloria

TREE OF LOVE

MATERIALS NEEDED

Flower pot
Dirt, clay, or plaster of Paris
Small branch
Small slips of paper
Pens
Yarn or ribbon

- Invite a grandparent (or pair of grandparents) for dinner.

- Make a centerpiece that looks like a small tree. This could be a branch anchored in plaster of Paris, or a small plant that resembles a tree; use your imagination.

- Give each family member five slips of paper on which he is asked to write five reasons why his grandparent is special: "I love Grandpa because . . ." or "I love Grandma because . . ."

- Sign each slip, and roll it up like a scroll. Tie it with a colorful ribbon and then attach it to the branches.

- Before dessert, have the grandparent(s) remove and read the slips aloud. Then watch for the sparkle in his or her eyes.

NAMES AND FACES

GRANDPARENTS' NAME CHART

- On a large piece of poster board, draw the first name of a grandparent in big, block letters, 6 or more inches tall, as space permits, arranging the letters vertically or horizontally.

- Inside the letters, draw colorful pictures of the grandparent's favorite foods, clothes, hobbies, sports, or games.

- If you choose to arrange the letters vertically, you may write an acrostic for each letter, naming the many positive qualities of the grandparent.

  EXAMPLE: E   elegant, effective, energetic

  L   loving, likable, laughing

  S   sacrificial, sensible, sweet

  A   admirable, attentive, adventuresome

ORIGINAL PORTRAITS

- Have each child draw a picture of the family, including the grandparent(s) in the picture.

- On the bottom of the picture have each child write what the grandparent(s) means to his family.

- Mail or give the picture to the grandparent(s).

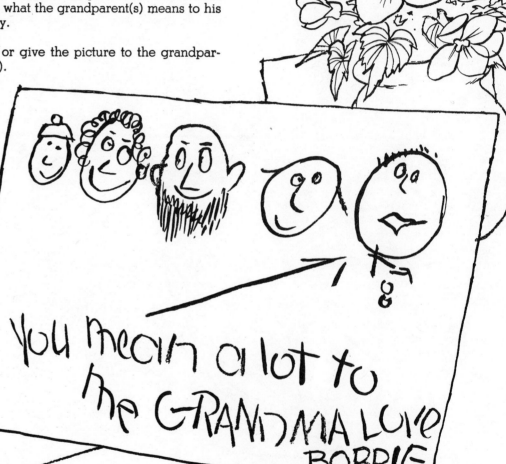

LOVE LETTERS*

As soon as a grandbaby is born, begin to write letters to him or her regularly—every month, every other month, twice a year, etc.

- Tell the child about his/her new abilities or physical development and the joy you feel in watching him/her grow.

- Assure the child of your love.

- Tell the child a little about yourself at this time, and a little about his/her parents.

- Mention the current national events.

NOTE: Parents will want to keep these treasures for the child to enjoy later when he/she is more able to appreciate them. They are good "builder-uppers" when a child is feeling discouraged, ugly, awkward, or afraid of a new situation. This is a good way to keep communications open at every age.

*Special thanks to Joyce Landorf for sharing this "memory maker" with us.

Dear Jamie
first day and
you looked at
to know that
most wonderful
years to come
as you today.
Love
Grandmother

GRANDPARENTS / GRANDCHILDREN

FAMILY

A LIVING WELCOME

In honor of a new baby, make a family project of planting a new tree that will grow as baby grows.

You will need:

a young tree (this may be a home grown seedling or a balled-and-burlapped tree from a nursery)
spades
small bag of peat moss
water
one fertilizer spike formulated for the type of tree you've chosen

- Choose a site for the tree that will allow plenty of room for growth and spreading. Be realistic; notice the size of full-grown trees of this species, or ask your nurseryman for information.

- Dig a hole approximately 1½ times as wide and as deep as the balled roots or twice as large as the root system of a seedling. Take turns digging, letting younger children help too.

- Sprinkle a good layer of peat moss in the bottom of the hole.

- Set the tree into the hole, letting the bottom of the roots touch the peat moss. If the roots are not balled, be sure to gently spread them, taking care to see that they are not broken or crowded.

- Check to see that the crown of the root system or the top of the balled roots is just slightly lower than the top surface of the ground.

- Fill the hole half full of water.

- Sprinkle loose soil into the hole until the hole is filled. As you fill, form a sort of saucer around the tree trunk that will hold water.

- Carefully water the tree again, filling the saucer but not so full that it runs over. As the water seeps in, it will naturally pack the soil around the roots so you will not need to press the soil down and run the danger of breaking the tender roots. After the water has seeped in, you may need to add a little more soil, but be sure to maintain the saucer.

- Insert one fertilizer spike just inside the rim of the soil saucer.

- Water each day by filling the saucer with water until the tree has a good start; then water whenever the weather is dry.

When the baby grows old enough to understand, tell him or her about the tree and that it was planted by those who love him or her most. Thank God for the joy of working with Him in the creation and nurturing process. Thank Him together for the new life that has come to be a part of your family. Promise to nurture each other through the "seasons" of your lives.

VARIATION

Make a tradition of planting a tree for each child in the family when he or she reaches age six (or whatever age you desire).

You may want to plant the same variety of tree each time—all pines, all hardwoods, fruit trees for an orchard, etc. Give the child in whose honor the tree is planted the responsibility of keeping it watered until it has a good start.

- Take a picture of the tree as it is being planted and keep it in a scrapbook.

- Take pictures periodically of the tree's growth.

- After the tree begins to mature, take pictures of it at different seasons.

- When the child is older, invite him or her to write about the tree. Add this writing to the scrapbook as well.

NEW BABY WELCOME BANNER

To welcome a new baby to the world, make a baby banner. This is a great activity for fathers to do with the other children in the family while Mom is at the hospital with the new baby. It is also a good project for the family to do together while waiting for a baby who is to be adopted.

- Obtain a large sheet of poster board or sheet of banquet table paper.

- Spread a protective layer of newspapers on the floor or the driveway.

- Let the children create a design and choose a slogan.

- Pencil it onto the banner.

- Use Magic Markers or tempera paints to create a colorful message. Have fun, and share the clean-up.

- Hang the banner over the crib in the baby's room.

SUGGESTIONS FOR BANNER SLOGANS

Welcome to the Fortner Family!
You're with Us, Baby!
You Can Voice Your Opinion Here!
It's Time for Timothy!
Building Site: Tommy Growing Here!
Sherri Is Something Special!
Patty's a Promise!

DAD'S TREAT

Here are some special things for fathers to do with kids:

- Pack a "Dad's Day" picnic and go to a surprise place to eat it.

  a park
  an empty lot
  the woods
  a lake

- Take son or daughter for a "dad-type" shopping trip to find *one* special item:

  a doll
  a new part for an electric train
  a model to build
  drumsticks or guitar strings
  a new dress
  tennis shoes
  first basketball or first baseball mitt

  Have lunch together afterward at a fancy place or favorite hamburger shop.

- Plan a "dad's special outing" with another father and son or daughter:

  go to a ballgame
  go to a car race
  go to a wrestling match
  take a nature hike
  go mountain climbing
  take a fishing trip

- Rent a movie or video tape from the library or from a rental store. Dads might enjoy sharing with the family:

  nature films
  live concerts by family favorites
  music groups
  old home movies taken when parents or kids
    were younger

- Make it dad's task to wake the kids up every morning by rubbing their backs or singing a silly wake-up song, or by raising the blinds and saying, "This is the day the Lord hath made!"

FAMILY

FAMILY

APPRECIATION TIME

HELPING HANDS

- Trace Mother's, Dad's, or grandparents' hands on a folded piece of 8½" x 11" paper. Draw one hand on the front of the paper and one on the back; the inside of the folded paper will be used for a message (see below).

- Let the child color the hand picture, drawing in the parent's watch, ring, fingernails, etc.

- Help the child compose a note to put inside the paper that shows appreciation for the loving things that are done by the person whose hands have been traced: fixing dinner, ironing, putting on Band-Aids, making repairs on the house, fixing toys, reading stories, etc.

- At the bottom of the page, write, "We appreciate you, Mom (Dad, Grandpa, etc.)!"

- Give as a special occasion card.

FAMILY CARD FOR MOTHER'S DAY/ FATHER'S DAY

- Fold a large sheet (12" x 18") of construction paper in half.

- Decorate the front of card with a greeting or picture. If the parent has a hobby, perhaps a picture related to that activity would be appropriate.

- Glue a snapshot of each person in the family inside the card and have each person write a message of love under his/her picture. These messages might all begin "You're special to me because . . ." or "One reason I love you so is . . ." or "I remember when you. . . ."

THANK YOU FOR "ME"

It's fun for a child to receive gifts on his or her birthday, but it will be even more meaningful to Mother to receive something special from the child whose birthday it is.

- On *your* birthday, send a corsage, bouquet of flowers, card, or other remembrance to your mother.

- Include a note saying, "Thank you for giving birth to me."

FAMILY

PROMISE COUPONS

For Father's Day or Mother's Day, make a coupon book filled with some promises to give the gift of yourself in time and energy to do helpful things. These coupons may be used any time in the next year.

- Cut blank index cards into equal coupon-size pieces.

- On each card write "This coupon good for . . . ," naming one chore or favor:

  doing dinner dishes one time
  cleaning the garage
  raking leaves for one hour
  one car wash
  one hour of window washing
  one hour of playing Scrabble (or other game of your choice)
  one week of feeding the dog

- Save one coupon piece to make an attractive cover for the coupon book.

- Staple all the coupons together and put the coupon book in an envelope.

- Tie a ribbon around the envelope and lay it on the parent's plate before dinner or breakfast of the special day.

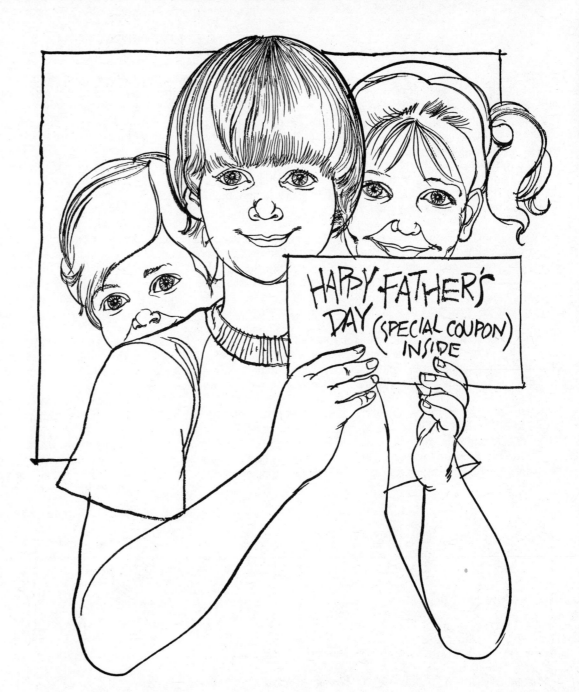

SEVENTEEN

The first day of school didn't start until one o'clock, so there was plenty of time for breakfast at McDonald's and shopping for the supplies that had been listed in the *Times-Tribune* the Wednesday before. You reminded us to go to McDonald's for breakfast. "We've always gone there on the first day of school," you said. Something hard to label stirred inside me when you said it. Perhaps it was pride—pride that you still found joy in our crazy little tradition; or perhaps it was pleasure—pleasure in knowing that you still choose to be with our family when you have your "druthers." But there was a certain sadness, too, and I couldn't stop the knowing this was your last first day of school.

You came down the stairs that morning all neat and well-groomed, the healthy glow of your summer tan and freckles still showing through your make-up, your sun-bleached hair carefully arranged. "Hi, Mom!" you said, and your grin showed your straight, white teeth. No more orthodontist appointments, I thought, and no more broken glasses to glue before school. Contacts and braces had sure been worth it.

"I've got to have my senior pictures taken tomorrow after school, Mom. Can I use the car?" "As far as I know," I answered, then reminded you of your promise to take your sister to get her hair trimmed at three o'clock that afternoon. Your driver's license had come in handy, too.

By then Amy and Benjy were ready, and we all piled into the car and drove to McDonald's. As we ate, we talked about other first days—the first day of kindergarten, the first day of junior high, and that scary first day in the big new high school. You all interrupted each other with stories of embarrassing moments, awards, friendships, and fright.

After we had eaten, we hurried to buy notebook paper and compasses before I dropped you all at school—first Amy and Benjy at the middle school, then you. " 'Bye, Mom," you said as you scooted across the seat. Then you stopped a moment and looked back over your shoulder. "And, Mom . . . thanks." It was the remnant of a kiss good-bye. It was the hesitancy of a little girl in ringlets beginning kindergarten. It was the anticipation of a young woman confident of her direction—these were all there in that gesture.

"I love you," was all I answered, but I had hoped that somehow you could hear with your heart the rest of the words that were going through my mind—words that told you how special you are to us; words that would let you know how rich your father and I have been because you came into our lives; words that tell you how much we believe in you, hope for you, pray for you, thank God for you. As the school doors closed behind you and you disappeared into the corridor, I wanted so to holler after you: *Wait! We have so much yet to do. We've never been to Hawaii. We've never taken a cruise. That book of poetry we wrote together isn't published yet. And what about the day we were going to spend at the cabin just being still and reading? Or the writers' workshop we planned to attend together in Illinois? You can't go yet . . . WAIT!"*

But I knew you couldn't wait, and that we could never keep you by calling a halt to your progress. You had promises to keep.

The things we want to save, Jesus has said, must be let go of, for the things we hold most tightly will be strangled in the end. And so, though I knew this was a last first, I also somehow knew that it was a first in a whole lifetime of new beginnings . . . and I rejoiced!

YOU ARE SPECIAL

Children are special, and this is an extra special way to show them that they are.

- Tell the children *special* people are coming to dinner, people you love more than anyone in the world.

- Have the children bathe, put on their nicest dress clothes, and hide in their rooms "until the company comes."

- While preparing their favorite meal, set the table with your best linens, china, crystal, candles, and fresh flowers.

- Make crowns as place cards and print their names on them: "King Robert" or "Queen Kimberly."

- When the meal is ready, call them and tell them the company is here. When they run out and ask, "Where are they?", tell them, "*You* are the guests of honor." Treat them like royalty that evening. This is a beautiful way to say "I love you."

FAMILY

FAMILY

MY SPECIAL DINNER

- Once a month, have each child prepare the evening menu for the family. (If there are two children in the family, this will involve two evenings a month; if there are three children, three evenings will be required, and so on.)

- Let the child help you shop for the groceries and help prepare the food and design special table decorations.

- Suggest that it will be fun to keep the menu a secret from the rest of the family until dinnertime.

- Use this project as a means for the child to learn about nutrition, about the effort necessary to prepare meals, the expense of food, methods of attractive preparation, etc.

THE V.I.P.

- Choose a smooth block of wood, a beautiful rock, a slice of a small log, etc.

- Using wood-burning tools, enamel, or Magic Markers, write a V.I.P. message for Dad's or Mom's desk, kitchen window, motor home, or van.

- Grandparents, aunts, and uncles will be proud to have one of these too.

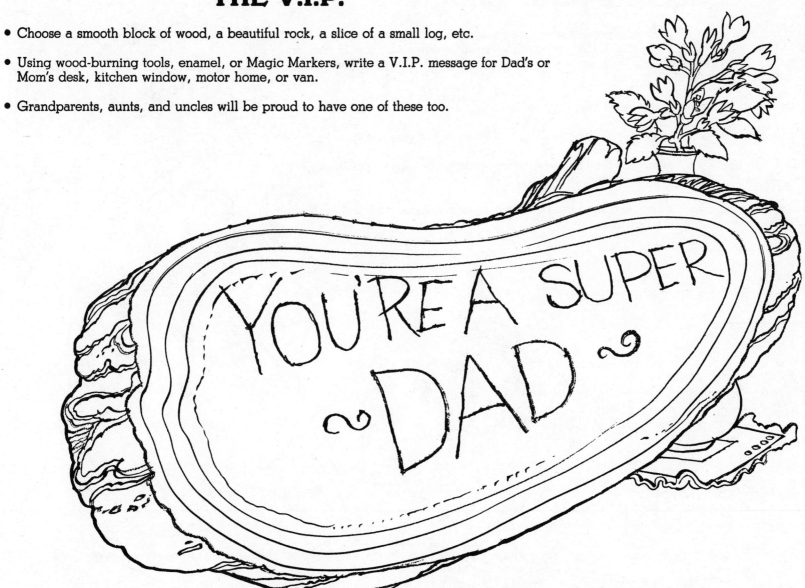

FAMILY

SECOND HONEYMOON

There is nothing better for kids than parents who love each other! Help parents stay in love by encouraging them to take a second honeymoon. Finding out where your parents went on their first honeymoon and whether they would enjoy going back to the same place might help you with your "promotion."

• Collect travel folders from the travel bureau.

• Volunteer to take extra responsibility for taking care of things while they are gone.

• Volunteer to give up something so they can use the money to go or plan a special project such as a garage sale to help make money.

• Go together with your brothers and sisters to buy Mom a new nightgown or some perfume and Dad some cologne or a new swimsuit.

KEEPING ROMANCE ALIVE

MONTHLY ANNIVERSARY

Here is a simple tradition that can help renew and keep alive your romantic relationship. Every month, on the day numbered the same as your wedding day, repeat a simple pattern; for instance, on the 10th of each month:

- Bring home a rose.

- Put a love note in the lunch pail.

- Go out for the evening, or promise a night out at a mutually agreed-upon time.

- Just whisper a question, worded the same way every month, such as "Do you know what day this is?"

A ROMANTIC TRAVEL TOUCH

- When going on an overnight trip or vacation, tuck a candle and an attractive candle-holder into your luggage.

- At bedtime, light the candle and enjoy the restful and soothing atmosphere. Candlelight adds a romantic touch to the surroundings whether you are in a motel or a camper.

- Make this a way of telling your spouse that he/she is loved and still romantically attractive to you.

"OUR SONG"

- Select a special love song that has meaning to both of you.

- Buy a record of that song or, if you have a piano or other instrument, learn to play it yourself.

- Hearing that song played and sung can often give your love an identity and help you through the ups and downs of everyday living.

HUSBANDS AND WIVES

HUSBANDS AND WIVES

KEEPING ROMANCE ALIVE (cont.)

THOUGHTFUL IDEAS FOR DAD

- A simple "thank you" kiss for Mom from Dad after a meal not only expresses gratitude to Mom, but it tells the kids that their parents love each other and appreciate each other.

- On your way home from work, pick up some bath crystals for your wife. Volunteer to care for the children while she leisurely enjoys her gift.

- If you have a new baby in your family, before your wife and new baby arrive home from the hospital, write a love note and leave it on the bedroom pillow. Welcome them home and pledge your love and care. The new mother will feel valued and will be pleasantly surprised. Then, tuck the message away in a keepsake file.

A TIME FOR JUST YOU AND ME

When Jim and I were first married, he was finishing his graduate training and I was busily teaching school. These career objectives forced us to postpone the experience of parenthood for a few years. We were extremely busy, but we were able to steal away for an occasional carefree weekend together. We would wander through department stores, holding hands, laughing and talking. We loved to window-shop for furniture and dream about how we hoped to decorate our house of the future. We would enjoy a light breakfast and then plan a candlelit dinner somewhere for the evening.

Many years have passed now—and such relaxing times are even more difficult to achieve. We still have a teenager at home who must be chauffeured hither and yon. And then, there are the pressures of Jim's work. God has blessed our ministry far more than we ever dreamed possible, but the demands are many. We take several trips during a typical year but usually with obligations to be faced upon arrival. I must admit there are times when I *long* for just the two of us to get away again and spend a relaxed, self-indulgent weekend together. This happened not too long ago.

Mammoth is a ski resort, six driving hours north of our house. After arranging for my mother to care for the children, we loaded the car and headed for our winter wonderland. I felt like a college girl again. We talked along the way and stopped to eat whenever it suited our fancy.

The next morning, we donned our colorful ski clothes and headed for our favorite restaurant, The Swiss Chalet. Hilda, the bubbly Swedish lady who owns the restaurant, calls me "Shoooolie." We love her.

Our conversation at the breakfast table took us into each other's worlds, again. Jim's eyes never looked bluer, and the love that's always there between us, steady and committed, surged to an emotional peak.

Driving to the ski lodge was equally exhilarating. The roads looked like a Currier and Ives Christmas card. The giant evergreens appeared majestic in their white fur coats. I knew it was going to be a great day for skiing. The sky was blue and the snow was a skier's paradise. Once on the mountain, we swished back and forth across the mountain like two adolescents. The snow was so "forgiving" we could do nothing wrong.

We were wonderfully exhausted driving back to the condo. Jim prepared a cozy fire in the fireplace while I made our favorite meal of fried burritos. We set up a card table and ate dinner by the firelight, discussing the good and bad skiing techniques of our day and an endless variety of other topics.

After the dinner dishes were cleaned up, we pulled the pillows off the couch, chose some of our favorite records and put them on the stereo. While relaxing by the fire, we promised each other we would try to repeat this private rendezvous at least once a year.

Believe me, the memories of that weekend motivated me for days afterward to be the wife and mother I needed to be.

As important as traditions are in a family, husbands and wives need romantic involvement when they are alone—a time when the children are not even thought of. This is good therapy not only for busy adults, but for their kids as well.

NEIGHBORS

FLOWER FESTIVAL

- Buy flowering bedding plants—marigolds, petunias, geraniums, or other favorites—or start your own from seed.

- Go as a family to someone you love and work together to fill his/her outside planters or window boxes.

  NOTE: If your friend has no containers, this annual activity could begin with the gift of a container.

- Follow these steps:

  1. Fill container with soil and mix in suitable fertilizer.

  2. Carefully separate plants and arrange them in container, giving attention to expected height and color of plants.

  3. Water carefully.

  4. Clean up any spilled soil, and carry away empty plant cartons.

- After the planting is done, share some lemonade.

BLOCK PARTY

A block party is a great way for neighbors to get acquainted, and one which creates a good neighborhood feeling. You can organize a simple get-together on your own for a starter. After the ice is broken, the whole group of neighbors will probably want to share in making a block party an annual affair, with a committee to choose a place, a date, and a time, and to coordinate a menu and other responsibilities. For a simple block party:

• Invite each family on the block to come to your house, bringing their own favorite dessert.

• Provide stick-on name tags (unless your neighborhood has been so stable that everyone knows each other).

• Arrange for a get-acquainted mixer (if neighbors are not well known to each other) or other fun group activity such as charades or a fast game of volleyball. You might want to try the popular icebreaker described below, which is sure to get everyone acquainted. The object is to have all of the guests introduce themselves to each other and to learn a little about each person.

WHAT'S MY NAME ICEBREAKER

1. Draw a chart of 1" to 2" squares on a sheet of paper. Make at least one square per guest.
2. At the top of each square write in a characteristic that could possibly fit one of your guests. (See suggestions below.) These can be designed to be humorous, or, if practical, the chart can be prepared to provide an interesting fact about each guest, making sure no one is omitted.
3. When guests arrive, provide each one with a pencil and a copy of the chart. Explain that they are to circulate among the group, meeting as many people as possible and asking questions that will help them fill in the blanks on the chart.
4. When the allotted time is up, find out who has the most squares filled in and ask him/her to read aloud the name and corresponding statement in each of the squares. Have each person stand as his/her name is called. If not all the guests have been introduced in this way, have the remaining ones stand and introduce themselves individually.

Talks back to TV commercials	Can wiggle ears	Can touch palms to floor
Has a hole in the bottom of his shoe now	Hates hamburgers	Runs 15 miles or more a day

TRAVELING FRIENDSHIP BASKET

Starting a Traveling Friendship Basket on its way through your neighborhood offers a good way to "reach out and touch" each other in friendship.

- Buy a large, inexpensive basket.

- Tie a cheerfully colored ribbon on it, along with directions asking the recipient to send it on to its next destination.

- The family starting the basket prepares the contents with their next-door neighbors in mind. For example: if the basket will be going to a family with children, fill it with brownies; if the basket is to go to a widow, fill it with a beautiful bouquet from your flower garden; if you sew, send it along with a practical creation for the home.

- The recipients are then asked to pass the basket to the neighbors on the other side of them (not the neighbors from whom they received the basket), again trying to fill it with contents appropriate for that neighbor or items that represent the special talents of the new donors.

- Keep the basket moving. Try not to let more than a week go by before sending it on.

- When the basket reaches the end of the block, send it to the family across the street and move it in the opposite direction so that it travels in a continuous circuit. The distance it travels can be greater than one block, of course, but it may be helpful to establish some kind of limit.

ESPECIALLY FOR FAMILIES TO DO WITH AN OLDER NEIGHBOR

Many older people have lost a spouse or close friends and also have more difficulty getting out than they did when they were younger. This can be a lonely time. Include them in some of your activities! Here are some ways:

- Invite your friend to go along with your family to the Dairy Queen, or drop by with an ice cream cone if he/she can't get out.

- Drop by now and then when you or your family are out riding bikes.

- Invite your friend to your birthday party. Make sure he/she has a hat to wear and a horn to blow like everyone else.

- Volunteer to mow the grass, clip around lamp posts, pull some weeds, or paint the mailbox.

- Mail unexpected notes or cards—valentines, Easter cards, school pictures, etc.

- Share a tape recording (provide a cassette player if needed) of a concert, church service, school program, band recital, etc.

- Ask your friend's opinion of a paper, a poem, or song you've written.

- Drop by with one or two of your friends so that your friend can meet them. Make your visits short.

- Offer to pick the cherries, sweep the driveway, wash the car, clean the windows on the outside, shake the rugs, run an errand.

Some of your neighbors, especially elderly ones, may have weak or blind eyes. Offer to provide "eyes" for them by volunteering to do the following things:

- Have a "read-in" once or twice a week. Suggest to the friend for whom you are reading that he/she invite other friends to share in the "read-in." Choose a "book-of-the-month" that all will enjoy having read aloud.

- Volunteer to write and mail letters or to help with the correspondence involved in paying bills.

- Give a subscription to a large-print edition of a good magazine such as *Reader's Digest* or *Guideposts*. Order from:

Reader's Digest Fund for the Blind
Large-Type Publication
P.O. Box 241
Mt. Morris, IL 61054

Guideposts
Big Print Edition
Carmel, NY 10512

GOOD FEELINGS

Helpers like the mailman, gardener, police-man, fireman, and others contribute much to the well-being of the neighborhood. Show appreciation and encourage good feelings.

- On a hot summer day, prepare a cool glass of punch or lemonade to give to the mailman when he comes, to the gardener who is working outside, to the policeman who walks the beat in your neighborhood, etc.

- A neighbor who is doing outdoor chores on a hot day will also appreciate a refreshing cold drink or even a brief helping hand. A moment of thoughtfulness builds good feelings among neighbors.

UNUSUAL WAYS TO SAY "GET WELL"

LEAVES OF LOVE

- On poster board, draw a large tree with bare limbs only.

- Cut out 10 to 20 leaves from green or multi-colored construction paper. Make them large enough to write on.

- Have each family member write a love note, joke, or riddle on a leaf. Repeat until all the leaves are used. Pin the leaves on the branches.

- Hang the tree in the patient's room. Be sure to place it where he/she can read it easily.

SNAPSHOT OF CHEER

Instead of taking or sending candy or flowers to a loved one or neighbor who is in the hospital, stop by the patient's home with your camera and take several pictures of his/her family. Have the film developed and printed and give the pictures to the patient. He/she will love showing them to the nurses and other friends who drop by, and your thoughtfulness will be much appreciated.

LEAVES OF LOVE

PEOPLE WHO ARE ILL

PEOPLE WHO ARE ILL

HOMEY COMFORTS FOR A SICK CHILD

Sick days—and nights—are no fun. Help them pass faster for your child.

- Read aloud the child's favorite books.

- To soothe a fever, dampen a washcloth with cold water, squeeze it out thoroughly, and place it on the patient's forehead.

- Sleep in the room with the child when there is a possibility of his/her vomiting, which can be a frightening experience for a child.

- When the child's stomach has settled, a small amount of scraped apple may be offered.

   Cut top edge from the apple.
   With spoon tip, scrape the apple meat from inside the peel and feed it to the child.

- Make hot "milk-toast" and spoon-feed to the patient.

   Place one slice of buttered toast in a shallow bowl. Pour steaming hot (but not boiled) milk over toast.

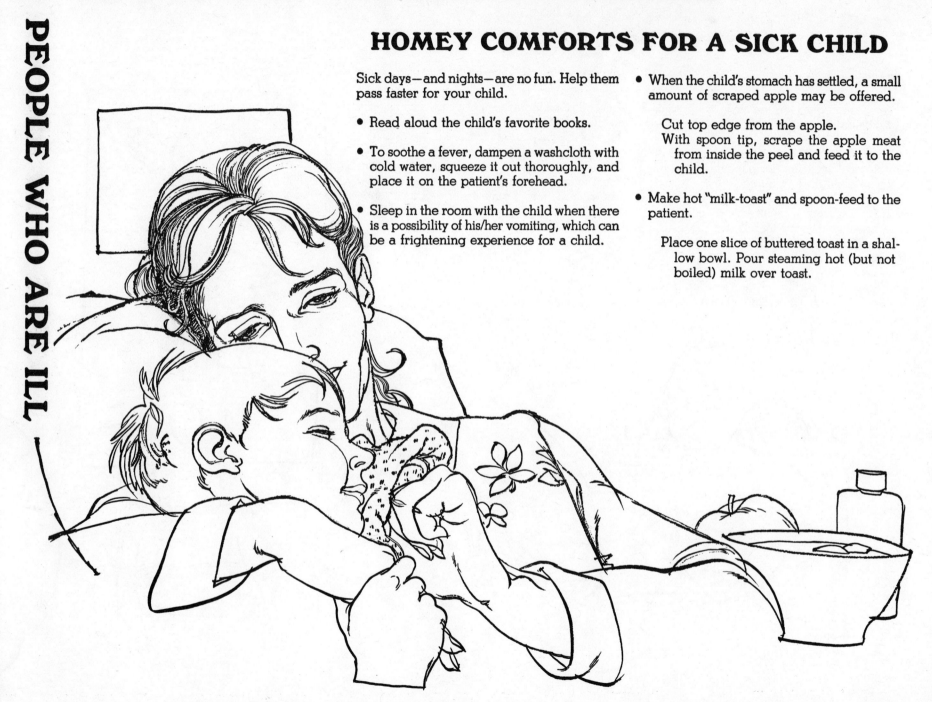

LAP TABLE

It is sometimes difficult to keep an active child as quiet as he/she needs to be during a minor illness or recuperation from something more serious. A lap table is a big help.

- Make a lap table from a cardboard box with arches cut out of it to enable the box to fit over a child's legs.

- Spray paint the table with a bright color and allow it to dry thoroughly.

- Turn the lap table upside down. There should be ample room to place a smaller box (a shoebox is a good size) inside the lap table to be used as a sick day busy box.

- Fill the box with suitable craft materials.

  newspapers (to protect the bed)
  scissors
  paste or Elmer's glue
  bits of yarn
  buttons
  crayons or felt markers
  small pieces of cloth
  construction paper
  magazines with lots of pictures (for cutting up)
  small package of tissue

- Use the box and lap table for craft activities only. Keep it put away until needed.

- When the lap table is needed, remove the inside box and place it within easy reach of the child. Place the lap table over his/her lap.

- Suggest things for the child to make—collages, puzzles, scrapbooks, drawings, etc. He/she will stay quietly busy for hours.

SUGGESTION: Lap tables make a great family gift for anyone who is ill. The shoebox insert can be filled with "grown-up" articles such as lip balm, body lotions, powder, Kleenex, comb, mirror, etc., as well as craft items or writing materials desired by the patient.

IDEAS FOR CHILDREN WITH A PROLONGED ILLNESS

- Send a small gift each day through the mail—a piece of gum, bookmark, balloon, package of plant seeds, miniature puzzle, lollipop, etc.

- Fill a variety box with the materials for making drawings, collages, posters, and constructing small objects: scissors, crayons, paper, pins, material, buttons, needles, thread, magnifying glass, mirror, pieces of aluminum foil, flashlight, box of paper clips, clay, paper hole-punch, toothpicks, glue, gummed stars, stickers, etc.

- Plant a garden indoors. Place two or three pieces of dampened cotton in a glass. Push a grapefruit seed, a pea, or a bean into the cotton. Keep cotton moist and watch the sprout grow!

JUST WHAT THE DOCTOR ORDERED

Fill a tiny cardboard box (approximately 2" x 2" x 1") with capsules of "medicine for the spirit."

- Buy large empty gelatin capsules at a pharmacy.

- Cut strips of colored paper slightly narrower than the length of the capsule and about four inches long.

- Write or type on each paper some personal word of encouragement, a Bible verse, or some other quotation.

- Roll up each strip of paper as tightly as possible, and insert it into one of the empty gelatin capsules.

- Fill the box with capsules and give it to the patient with instructions to "take" a capsule every four hours, three times a day, or on a schedule that will fit the probable length of the patient's stay in bed.

EXAMPLE: "You're the best sister a guy could have. I love you."

"When you get well, I promise to treat you to an ice cream cone at Barkley's."

"Thanks for all the times you've helped me with my math. I'm glad you're so smart!"

"My heart shall rejoice in thy salvation" (Ps. 13:5).

"I will sing unto the Lord for He hath dealt bountifully with me" (Ps. 13:6).

"The Lord is my light and my salvation; whom shall I fear? The Lord is the strength of my life; of whom shall I be afraid?" (Ps. 27:1).

PEOPLE WHO ARE ILL

WHEN YOU'RE FEELING BETTER

BAKED PLAY DOUGH COOKIES

- Give the child a cookie sheet, play dough (recipe below), and a few cookie cutters.

- Cut out play dough cookies and place on the baking sheet. Bake.

- Cool and decorate the cookies with poster paint or marker pens.

PLAY DOUGH RECIPE

4 cups flour
1 cup salt
1½ cups water (add more if needed)
(For colored dough, add a few drops of food coloring to the water)

Bake at 325 degrees for 2 to 3 hours until dough is hardened.

NOTE: This mixture is *not* to be eaten, but is intended for crafts only.

PITCH A PENNY

- Place a large can on the floor near the sick child's bed.

- Give the child a handful of pennies.

- Have him see how many pennies he can pitch into the can.

MAKING MEMORIES IN GOD'S WORD

GOD'S WORD / LIGHT

"JESUS IS LIGHT"

- Place a candle on the table for a centerpiece. Let the candle provide the *only* light for the meal.

- Have one family member read aloud Isaiah 9:2–7. Talk about how the world was in darkness before He came. Jesus brought light; Jesus *is* light.

- Discuss the fact that most people in the world even today have less light than we do. Many have no electricity but use candles or oil lamps.

- Point out also that most of the world has not heard the gospel, as we have in this country.

- Pray a special prayer about light. Use this one or one of your own:

Thank You for the light of the gospel. Help us send it to the world's dark places as well as to those who live in darkness all around us.

OBJECT LESSON IN GOD'S WORD

- Prepare an obstacle course in a hallway, using toys, chairs, books, and boxes placed in such a way as to make it difficult to get through.

- Turn off all the lights.

- In turn, let each family member walk or crawl through the hallway.

- Next, let someone lead the way with a flashlight.

- Turn on the lights. Discuss how it felt to get through the maze in the dark. Was it difficult? How did you feel with the flashlight?

- In the Bible, turn to Psalm 119:105 and John 8:12. Read the verses aloud.

- Discuss how God's Word can lead us through the "dark places" in life; how it "lights" our path and gives us direction.

GOD'S WORD / LIGHT

TWENTY QUESTIONS

Play this familiar game choosing a biblical character or object as the secret to be guessed.

- Draw straws to determine who will be "it," the person who chooses the secret.

- Have the other members of the family guess who or what the secret is by asking twenty questions that can be answered by a simple yes or no.

- Each family member asks one question in turn.

- Whoever guesses correctly before the twentieth question becomes "it," and gets the next turn to choose a secret.

- If no one guesses the secret in twenty questions, the person who is "it" is the winner, and he or she chooses another person to be "it."

LEARNING GOD'S WORD TOGETHER

- Choose a Bible verse to memorize.

- Have someone in the family circle say the first word of the verse.

- Continue around the circle with each person saying the next word until the verse has been completed.

- Each time the verse is rehearsed, start with a different family member until each person has learned the verse.

- This is also a fun way to learn the names of the books of the Bible.

GOD'S WORD / MEMORY LEARNING

THE BIBLE ALPHABET

- To do this activity, choose a special day of the week that will suit your family.

- Have each member of the family choose and memorize a Bible verse that begins with the letter *A*. The verse that is chosen must be a complete sentence.

- At a certain time of day (breakfast, supper, bedtime, or whatever time the family chooses) have each person recite his/her verse.

- The next week, learn verses beginning with *B*, and the following week learn verses beginning with *C*, and so on.

- Every third or fourth day, review verses already learned to see how far through the alphabet each person can go. Keep this a fun time.

- Continue the activity until everyone can complete the alphabet. The REAL fun begins with letters like X and Z.

EXAMPLE VERSES: A—All have sinned and come short of the glory of God (Rom. 3:23).

B—Believe on the Lord Jesus Christ and thou shalt be saved (Acts 16:31).

C—Choose ye this day whom ye will serve (Josh. 24:15).

D—Delight thyself also in the Lord (Ps. 37:4).

WORD CUP

The object of this game is to recall a Bible verse based on a key word that is contained in the verse or that pertains to the thought of the verse. This game is ideal for mealtime or anytime the family is gathered together.

- Print "key" words on slips of paper or tiny squares of poster board. (The cardboard that backs paper napkin packages is perfect.)

- Put the words in a teacup or mug.

- Pass the cup around the dinner table asking each person (guests, too) to take one word.

- At the end of dinner, ask each person to take a turn recalling a verse from the Bible (or an incident) that contains that word or speaks to that subject.

- Some words that might be used are:

  heart
  sin
  body
  liars
  worry
  children

- Suggested subjects could be:

  honesty
  obedience
  time management
  friends
  forgiveness

GOD'S WORD / MEMORY LEARNING

MYSTERY VERSE

- Choose a Bible verse.

- Write each word of the verse on a separate card.

- Spread the cards on the table in correct order.

- Remove three or four cards.

- See who can say the whole verse, filling in the "mystery" words from memory.

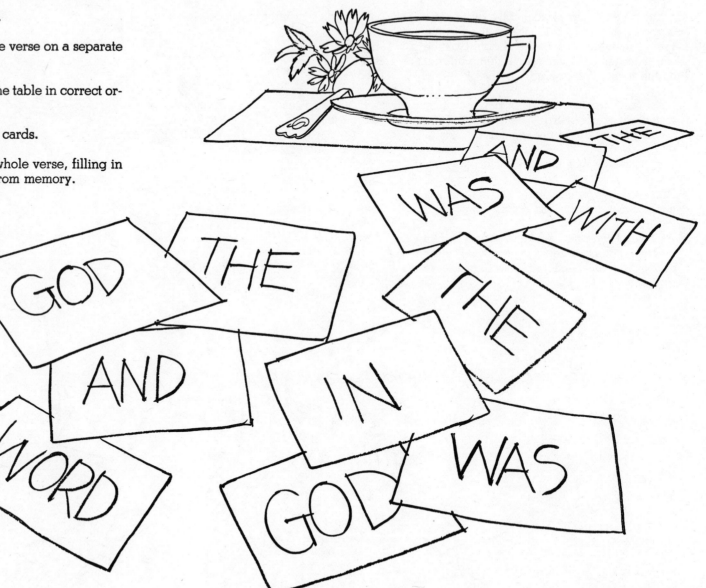

KEEPING MEMORIES ALIVE

TIME TO REMINISCE

- Before grown children arrive for a visit, get out things you made together or collected as they were growing up. Have these things displayed in a special room (den, living room, screened front porch, etc.). Some things might be:

  baby books and scrapbooks
  sports or achievement awards, report cards, medals, graduation dresses, first baseball uni-
    forms, first ice skates, etc.
  birthday flags (see p. 47, Special Days / Birthdays)
  New Year's diaries (see p. 18, Special Days / New Year's)
  summer memory books (see p. 98, Seasons / Summer)
  vacation diaries (see p. 139, Special Places / Vacations)
  soil diaries (see p. 133, Special Places / Vacations)
  memory collages (see p. 130, Special Places / Vacations)
  people prints (see p. 120, Special Places / The Water's Edge)

- Fill a big wicker basket full of popcorn and spend some happy hours remembering and cele- brating the gift of being a family.

BONUS: If there are grandchildren, this is a special time for them to get to know something about what their parents were like as children and what they did then.

FAMILY REUNION

Make this a very special occasion by sharing not only food but the reliving and creation of memories.

- Share a meal, each bringing his/her best dish.

- Have a short devotion including singing accompanied by piano, guitar, and/or other instruments played by family members.

- Go around the family circle, each person telling the most important thing that has happened in his/her life since all were last together.

- Have a "talent show" with at least one contribution from each grown child and/or the new family he/she represents and from each parent.

MEMORIES / KEEP ALIVE

THE FAMILY THAT PLAYS TOGETHER . . .

Play is just as important for adults in building and maintaining healthy relationships as it is for children. When the family clan is together, make time for play. Try any or all of the following:

- Table games such as Roll-a-Role, Strategy, Rook, Monopoly, Reunion.

- Puzzles (large, time-consuming jigsaw puzzles offer a wonderful opportunity for conversation).

- Outside games such as kickball, softball, volleyball, tennis, badminton, etc.

- Fishing and camping (even backyard camping).

- Sidewalk art contests. (Give everyone a dime store box of colored chalk with which to create a driveway or sidewalk "masterpiece." Have a neighbor judge the prettiest, funniest, most unique. The first rainstorm will erase the art, but for a few days you can enjoy the sidewalk gallery.)

- Ditch-um. (This is a team version of hide-and-go seek played at night from a "home base." Since the "seekers" are a team, young children can team up with the grownups and feel safe.)

- Roller skating party (on the sidewalks in your neighborhood, on a large driveway, at an empty parking lot, or at a roller rink).

- Sledding party (with hot chocolate and a warming bonfire).

- Clambake (see p. 135, Making Memories in Special Places / The Water's Edge).

SHARE A PROJECT

Save a special project to be done when grown children (and perhaps *their* children) come home. Here are some suggestions:

• Cut, saw and split a tree for the winter's supply of firewood. This is a great time to teach youngsters how to prepare firewood and at the same time share physical labor. A grown son or daughter and his/her father or mother could find this a good time for conversation, too.

• Plant something together: a tree, berry bushes, bulbs, fruit trees, etc. You should have ready:

    items to be planted
    fertilizer
    peat moss
    garden hose and spades (include small
        spades for children)

• Pick and prepare fruit or garden produce.

• Can, preserve, or freeze fruits and vegetables for winter:

    make apple butter, grape jam, peach pre-
        serves
    can green beans, tomatoes, beets, etc.
    freeze corn, squash, cherries, berries

Remember to include small children. They can shell peas, wash jars, snap beans, pick up boxes of wood chips, water plants, etc.

MEMORIES / KEEP ALIVE

MEMORIES / KEEP ALIVE

VIDEO VIRTUOSOS

If there is a video camera and recorder in the family, work together to create a TV pilot film. Brainstorm to come up with a plot. Then write a script; assign family members, old and young, to play the parts. You might need the following:

a writer
a producer
a director
a camera operator
actors
costume coordinator
makeup artist
technical director (who sees to details like providing fresh power packs, supplying cool drinks for actors, running errands, etc.)

Don't be afraid to let children take part in all these areas. They are very creative at inventing plots, and often know a great deal about television production.

Your show might be a mystery, drama, situation comedy, quiz show, or talk show. You will probably need to proceed with the following steps:

• Create a script.

• Block out the scenes and scout the filming locations.

• Rehearse each scene.

• Film scenes in sequence (unless your equipment has editing capabilities).

To assure the success of this project, relax and have fun. Don't be afraid to try something crazy. The adults should not be too exacting or critical; remember, the idea is to "make a memory" that is *fun* for everyone.

LITERARY HERITAGE

Spend a rainy afternoon with the books and records you loved as you (or your children) were growing up. Play records of songs or stories; take turns reading little storybooks aloud, recalling events associated in your minds with those books or records. The little ones of the third generation will love this time, too.

Reread aloud as a family the great children's literature that has allegorical meaning to you now. Discuss the spiritual or moral applications that you now understand as an adult.

BOOKS

The Chronicles of Narnia by C. S. Lewis
Alice in Wonderland by Lewis Carroll
The Giving Tree by Shel Silverstein
Hope for the Flowers by Trina Paulus
Tom Sawyer and *Huckleberry Finn* by Mark Twain
Treasure Island by Robert Louis Stevenson
The Velveteen Rabbit by Margery Williams

NURSERY RHYMES AND POEMS

"There Was a Crooked Man," attributed to Mother Goose
"Mary Had a Little Lamb" by Sarah Josepha Hale
"Pussy Cat, Pussy Cat" by Christina Rossetti
"The Duel" by Eugene Field
"Swing Song" by William Allingham
"The Owl and the Pussycat" by Edward Lear

POETRY

"Thanatopsis" by William Cullen Bryant
"The Landing of the Pilgrim Fathers in New England" by Felicia Hemans
"A Thing of Beauty" by John Keats
"If" by Rudyard Kipling
"The Eternal Goodness" by John Greenleaf Whittier
The poems of Robert Louis Stevenson
"Two Roads" and "Stopping by Woods on a Snowy Evening" by Robert Frost
Poems by Henry Wadsworth Longfellow such as:
  "The Wreck of the Hesperus"
  "Psalm of Life"
  "Song of Hiawatha"
  "The Village Blacksmith"
  "I Heard the Bells on Christmas Day"

MEMORIES / KEEP ALIVE

MEMORY BOOK

Rather than keeping a "baby book," keep a Memory Book. Buy a blank book for each child and keep a sort of diary of that child's growth: physical, emotional, spiritual. Every few months (or weeks, if the child is very young) make an entry. You might include:

how they have grown
things they have learned
special experiences (bad moments as well as good moments)
how you felt about those moments
why that child is special
new events or things that are going on in the world at that time
special things the child says
special awards or honors, relating the event as a special family time

Give the book (or books) to the child as a gift when he / she is old enough to appreciate it. Some occasions for this gift might be:

sixteenth birthday
eighteenth birthday
high school graduation
college graduation
wedding day

SCRAPBOOK

Keep a scrapbook for each child in the family. Begin at birth and maintain it as long as possible. Include:

- Pictures as they grow.

- A picture of your house when the child was born (years later, the house will have changed—it might be a new color; additions may have been built; trees will have grown; etc.).

- Snapshots to show what parents, grandparents, siblings, cousins looked like when the child was born.

- Pictures of the child's first room or nursery.

- Written paragraphs of cute things he or she said, accounts of accidents and experiences.

- Pictures of holidays and memorable moments:

  first lost tooth
  first haircut
  first day of school
  first pumpkin carved for Halloween
  piano recitals, sports participation,
    speeches made
  news clippings
  original writing (stories, poems, etc.)
  best art effort at each age (if not drawing,
    take photos of sculptures, drama,
    craft items, etc.)

DANAE—THE APPLE OF OUR EYE . . .

When I was carrying our first child, my mother-in-law told me to expect a boy because, historically, the Dobsons rarely produced little girls. Jokingly she said she didn't think she'd even know *how* to care for a granddaughter. Jim was also expecting a boy, reminding me that six families in his parents' generation had borne only one female among many males. This made me want a little girl all the more. However, I decorated the nursery in yellow and white just to be safe.

Needless to say, we were delighted when our daughter, Danae, was born. Jim's mom was equally pleased (and yes, she learned how to take care of little girls remarkably well!).

Danae's early childhood was so exciting for Jim and me, as we watched the development of our creative and happy daughter. We lived on the most fertile street in Southern California, and an array of children incessantly knocked on our front door to play with Danae.

One day when she was about four years old, I decided to give Danae and her friends a tea party. I got out my special china from the cupboard and we planned a party complete with cookies and napkins. Danae helped me create pretend names for all her friends. There were Mrs. Perry, Mrs. White, Mrs. Green, and I was Mrs. Snail (I didn't ask any questions!). The names stuck and everytime we decided to have a tea party in the future, I was Mrs. Snail.

Danae had always had a soft place in her heart for animals, whether real or stuffed. As a small child, she would place her dolls on a shelf and role-play with her teddy bears, stuffed rabbits, and kittens. Each one had a special name and would take its turn sleeping with her. She is eighteen now and a freshman in college, and although her furry friends no longer have a little girl to play with, they sit in her room as a silent reminder of the precious childhood which is now history.

I admit that it has been difficult for me to see Danae grow up. Oh, I know that she could not remain a child, and I wouldn't want to freeze her development at an immature age. But I loved every minute of her childhood and cherish the memories we created during those happy years.

I worked hard on the task of "letting go" of Danae during her last three years at home. Sometimes that involved the most difficult assignment of all: permitting her to experience the painful consequences of irresponsibility and immaturity.

One such incident occurred when she was fifteen years of age. Danae had stayed up far too late one night and then could not pull herself out of bed the next morning. This had happened several times before, and each time I had rescued her by helping get things together and then driving her to school. Jim and I agreed, however, that it was time for Danae to accept *full* responsibility for getting to school before the tardy bell rang.

On this particular morning, Danae was running hopelessly behind. When her carpool ride arrived and the driver honked, she came flying out of the shower, draped in a towel, and asked me if I'd please wave them on—she wasn't going to make it. Quite obviously! I stuck my head out the door and gave them the "good-by" sign. I was involved in a class at that time myself and was in the process of getting ready to leave.

In approximately forty-five minutes, with bed made and the bathroom straight, a beautifully groomed fifteen-year-old appeared at my door and said, "Uh . . . Mom, it's almost time for my algebra class. I can't walk because these shoes hurt my feet."

I ignored the hint and said, "Well, take them off and put on your tennis shoes and just before you get to school, switch back."

"Oh, Mother!" she said. "I couldn't do that. Do you realize how ridiculous this pleated skirt would look with tennis shoes?"

I said, "Well, I guess you have a problem then," and continued combing my hair.

Danae said, "Do you think I could make it on time if I rode Ryan's skateboard to school?"

Now, she and I both knew that there was *no way* she intended to ride her ten-year-old brother's skateboard to school. A sophomore in high school arriving at school on a skateboard was unheard of. She would have suffered a barrage of adolescent ridicule from her classmates. She was hoping that I would weaken and drive her to school. Nevertheless, I responded to her proposal as if she were serious. Casually I said,

"Danae, it wouldn't matter what you rode to school, you couldn't make it in ten minutes. Besides, you'd better check with Ryan before you borrow his skateboard."

She turned around with a "woe is me" look on her face and walked away. Pretty soon I heard her shuffling down the hall again.

"Uh . . . Mom, how much do you think it would cost to get Dial-a-ride out here?" (Dial-a-ride is the name of our city-sponsored cab company.)

I said, "I don't know, Danae. You'll have to check it out."

She made a hasty call and then returned to say, "Good! It's only 75 cents and Dad owes me a dollar on my allowance. They'll be here in ten minutes."

Danae gathered up her books and went out in front of the house and sat on the curb with her head down, waiting for Dial-a-ride. I was then faced with one of the most difficult assignments I've experienced. I backed my car out of the driveway and left my beloved teen-age daughter sitting dejectedly on a curb. As I drove off, my mind was flooded with all the horrible things that can happen to a young girl sitting alone on the edge of a street: what if the cab driver never took her to school, and other similar thoughts. I lifted my teary eyes up to my Heavenly Father and I said, "Lord, You know I'm trying to be a good parent. I'm hoping to teach Danae responsibility through this experience, but it's so difficult. Would You send a guardian angel to watch over her and get her to school safely?"

The Lord heard my prayer, for she came bounding into the house after school, threw her books on the table, flung herself across the counter and wailed, "Oh, Mother! How embarrassing! How horrible! Do you know what kind of cab Dial-a-ride has? It is *a huge, old, beat-up* station wagon. The driver drove me right up in front of the school and all my friends saw me. Oh (groan), I will never do that again!" (Ah, poetic justice.)

Not risking another disastrous episode, Danae was up at the crack of dawn the next morning with the shower blasting. We both profited from the stresses of that encounter with irresponsibility.

It is extremely difficult for loving, caring parents to let their vulnerable kids face embarrassment or failure—especially when they could so easily "bail them out" in moments of irresponsibility. Nevertheless, there is value to be derived from painful or stressful consequences. Even the inevitable conflict that occurs between adolescent and parent can be beneficial. I remember bumping heads with Danae later that same year over a bad attitude that she was revealing. We stood toe to toe and flung harsh accusations at one another, followed by guilt (mine) and further rebellion (hers). I felt like I had "blown it" to let my emotions get so out of control, and left in the car to run some errands.

When I returned, I found a chocolate cake Danae had baked. Beside it was a note which read, "I'm sorry I was so difficult to get along with today, Mom. This cake is for you." A little love goes a long way to ease the pain of a frustrated mother. We ate the cake together and talked about how we could do better in the future.

The writer of the book of Hebrews fully understood the function of distress and even punishment in shaping our lives and helping us grow. It is beautifully stated in chapter 12, verses 7–11:

> Let God train you, for he is doing what any loving father does for his children. Whoever heard of a son who was never corrected? If God doesn't punish you when you need it, as other fathers punish their sons, then it means that you aren't really God's son at all—that you don't really belong in his family. Since we respect our fathers here on earth, though they punish us, should we not all the more cheerfully submit to God's training so that we can begin really to live?

> Our earthly fathers trained us for a few brief years, doing the best for us that they knew how, but God's correction is always right and for our best good, that we may share his holiness. Being punished isn't enjoyable while it is happening—it hurts! But afterwards we can see the result, a quiet growth in grace and character. (TLB)

FAMILY BULLETIN BOARD

Hang a family bulletin board in your kitchen, family room, or hallway. Each family member should have a section in which to share his/her:

achievements
talents
messages
snapshots

You might want to work together as a family on special seasonal displays:

Christmas
Valentine's Day
Autumn collages

CHRISTMAS AMBROSIA

A traditional Christmas dish for many families is Ambrosia. Often each of five different family units brings one ingredient and each family chooses one member to put that family's contribution into the Ambrosia bowl. If you have only two or three grown children, make up the other three ingredients by inviting an aunt and uncle, grandparent, or a neighbor to share in this special recipe.

Combine equal amounts of:

   snowflake coconut
   pineapple tidbits
   tiny marshmallows
   mandarin oranges (canned)
   seedless green grapes

The host mixes this with sour cream in a proportion of 1 cup sour cream to 10 cups of combined fruit ingredients. You may wish to add English walnuts to the fruit mixture.

TAFFY PULL

When the kids (and their kids) are home, have a taffy pull. Since this is such a good winter activity, it is perfect for Thanksgiving or Christmas, or the days after.
See p. 114 (Seasons / Winter) for a good molasses taffy recipe.

MEMORABLE MEMORY MAKERS

Mrs. Charlie (Martha) Shedd

Co-author with her husband, of *Celebration in the Bedroom*, and seminar co-leader, *Fun Family Forums*

Our family devotion is one of our fun traditions. And the fun is tied up in what we call "interesting things." We decided (by a family vote) that we would reserve the time immediately following dinner for this.

The first person (designated by dad) reports on his most interesting experience during that last twenty-four hours. This may include something unusual which happened to him or his friends . . . a good grade . . . a home-run . . . a compliment . . . some wonder of nature . . . the place where he felt God close . . . big breaks . . . bad breaks . . . little breaks in the routine . . . somebody's trauma . . . the good, the bad, the ugly; any of these will do.

Each person takes his turn around the table. No one is permitted to repeat what has been said before. After everyone has had one turn, seconds and thirds are admissible. All this leads to considerable traffic in ideas.

Several good things come from this practice.

1. Each person opens up his soul a little for all to see what's going on inside. During the "cave" years this is particularly important. In their early teens our children seemed to withdraw for a time. We call these the "cave" years. Since there is a twenty-five cent fine for the non-participant, everyone makes a noble effort. Families who feel a dearth of relationship will find "interesting things" a powerful stimulant.

2. "Serendipity" is another plus. The Persian story has it that those Princes of Serendip were forever reading

life for surprises. The practice of "interesting things" in our devotional base has affected us like that. We live with expectancy. Each day is vibrant with meaning. The goodness of God is never far away.

3. "Interesting things" also helps to keep the family conversation happy and positive. Instead of the usual gripes of five children about teachers, neighbors, friends, our conversation tends to be more varied and more upbeat.

Then our family worship closes with reading from a selected devotional—the Bible, children's Bible story book, a denominational guide, some book of meditations, or something the leader has read somewhere. Turns are taken in order by members of the family, and then the leader closes with prayer. We hold hands as he prays, or requests silent prayer, sentence prayers, the Lord's prayer.

Let's face it, we don't succeed 100 percent of the time, but our policy is to hang loose. We do better with plenty of leeway. When everyone is on a tight schedule, we may only say a quick prayer; or we have even been known to close on this note: "The Lord knows we're busy tonight—pray on the way."

The big thing is that it's a fun time, a time to celebrate.

Cordially,

Martha

Martha Shedd

Mrs. Dick (Joyce) Landorf

Author of *Irregular People, Joseph,* and others
Speaker and seminar leader

THE YEAR TO HAVE A BABY

When our children were very young and our finances were _very_ lean, we found that having a tree each Christmas did not blend into our budget. So we alternated years. One Christmas we'd have a decorated tree and the next we set up the crèche.

The first year we did this, I bought a little manger scene from the dime store, made a box stable covered with burlap, and took the children up the hill to get some beautiful rocks and pine branches. I cleaned off a corner end table, put the box, stones, branches and figures up and said, "Now this is the year of the baby"— and then proceeded to tell the children all about the birth of Jesus.

The only time it backfired was the year Laurie was old enough to tell all the neighbors that this year "we are having a baby." She failed to add "instead of a tree." So I had a good deal of explaining to do.

Now that Rick is a father and finances are tight they have their year of the baby too, so the tradition goes on.

NEVER SEND JUST A CARD

We have always been a note writing family. You could not leave our house without a small piece of paper on the desk saying where, when, what, and with whom. I've saved all of those priceless communiqués. They are a record of growth!

Also, we could buy a birthday card for birthdays, but it _always_ had to have a birthday letter in it. (After all, _anybody_ can buy a Hallmark card, but not everybody can write a letter.) Writing a birthday letter took time, discipline, and much thought. But even to this day, I get a real thrill when I open up a card and a letter in my children's handwriting drops out.

Joyce

Joyce

Miss Lillie Knauls

Singer, recording artist

My mom did domestic work for one of the bank executives. Each Christmas he would personally deliver a large box of fruit, nuts and candies to our house.

We were not what you might call a "poor" family; however, my parents did not give anything except practical gifts, and not many of them. They were more interested in having a gathering of the family and friends for a time of food (the only time we had "Ambrosia"—I LOVE IT!) and fellowship, than the giving and receiving of lots of gifts.

Consequently, I grew up believing that Christmas is Christ's birthday and not a time for going into debt to have gifts for everyone. I now like to buy and give gifts for no reason.

Lillie Knauls

One of the traditions which our family has carried on from Mort's parents (and hopefully our children will pass it along to their children) is the custom of reading the lovely story of Jesus' birth from the Gospel of Luke before opening our Christmas presents.

Grandparents, sisters, brothers, uncles, aunts, and cousins have all participated in this ritual over the years. Now, both grandfathers are gone, but how fortunate we are to have Mort's father, Pop Crim, and my father, Pop Dale, on tape reading the Christmas story to the family—which incidentally proved to be their last Christmas with us.

We think it is a beautiful tradition worth passing along to our children.

Sincerely,

Nicki

Mrs. Mort (Nicki) Crim

Wife of CBS News anchorman, WDIV-TV, Detroit

Elisabeth Elliot

Missionary, author, speaker
Widowed when her husband Jim Elliot was killed
by Auca Indians

I am grateful for family "prayers," which we had twice a day. In the morning after breakfast we all (six children and parents) went into the living room and sang a hymn. Either father or mother played the piano and we all sang, not skipping stanzas, and moving straight through a hymnbook, one hymn per day. As a result of this, all of us know hundreds of great old hymns by heart. There is no calculating the value of this treasury in my own spiritual progress.

Next to the Bible, hymns speak most deeply to my needs and daily experience. In times of great temptation and loneliness (in the jungle, for example) I have been sustained by those wonderful words, etched deeply in my mind in those malleable childhood years. You know how easily your children learn TV commercials. Why not stuff their minds with something much more lasting and profitable? Memorization is a snap for children.

I taught Valerie, my own daughter, hymns when we lived in thatched houses in the jungle, sitting on her bed with her just before she went to sleep. We had no piano, of course, and no family. Sometimes there were Indians around, marveling at the strange "noise" we made. I typed up many hymns from memory when I had no hymnbook, and bound some of them in a small booklet for her when she learned to read.

Scripture commands us to "speak to ourselves with psalms and hymns and spiritual songs." A family that sings builds a strong spiritual bond, and creates for each individual a priceless source of comfort and godly instruction which will always be there, whether he is in touch with other Christians or in a situation where such fellowship may be impossible.

Elisabeth Elliot

Mrs. Larry (Nordis) Christenson

Homemaker and grandmother
Wife of Director of the International Lutheran
Renewal Center

Children love things which happen again and again. These things can be little, even insignificant, but they grow to make a family feeling.

When the children were little, Larry invented the "hugging machine." He would take two or three, sometimes all four children on his lap at the same time. With each of them facing him and reaching to hug him, he would reach out to hug all of them at one time and would squeeze the squeals out of them. They loved the "hugging 'chine."

One of our oldest traditions is "cratch." It began when Tim, our oldest, was three years old. He was restless at bedtime, didn't want to stay in bed. Bedtime began to be an unhappy time. So one of us would sit by him on the bed, scratch and rub his back, and sing a hymn. That made it a happy, peaceful time, and gave Tim time to settle down and give up for the day. Laurie was not very old when she noticed this process and looking out between the slats of her crib, seemed to be saying, "What about me?" So for years we would "cratch" and sing about me?" So for years we would "cratch" and sing every night. Each child chose his/her favorite song for this time. The main quality which made it a favorite was that it was long. Some evenings we felt too busy, too tired, or too impatient to sit and scratch, but at these times we found that it took more time to explain why we were not doing it than to do it. So there were few evenings that it did not happen. They even taught the babysitter to do it.

A tradition that we imported from Germany, after having lived there a year is our mealtime greeting. After we pray grace together, we join hands around the table, look at each other, and say, "Blessed mealtime." Now, for our granddaughter, that is the highlight of the meal. It is precious to see that this gives her a feeling of belonging to something special—a family!

Nordis Christenson

Miss Corrie ten Boom

World-famous speaker and author (*The Hiding Place*, *Tramp for the Lord*, and others)

My security was assured in many ways as a child. Every night I would go to the door of my room in my nightie and call out, "Papa, I'm ready for bed." He would come to my room and pray with me before I went to sleep. I can remember that he always took time with us, and he would tuck the blankets around my shoulders very carefully, with his own characteristic precision. Then he would put his hand gently on my face and say, "Sleep well, Corrie . . . I love you."

I would be very, very still, because I thought that if I moved I might lose the touch of his hand; I wanted to feel it until I fell asleep.

Many years later in a concentration camp in Germany, I sometimes remembered the feeling of my father's hand on my face. When I was lying beside Betsie on a wretched, dirty mattress in that dehumanizing prison, I would say, "Oh, Lord, let me feel Your hand upon me . . . may I creep under the shadow of Your wings."

In the midst of that suffering was my heavenly Father's security.

Corrie ten Boom, In My Father's House (Fleming H. Revell Company, © 1976), p. 58, used by permission.

As our family gathered around the table for meals, one of my grandparents read from the Bible, usually three times a day. It was kind of spiritual dessert. They had enjoyed physical food from the hand of God; now they would enjoy spiritual food.

My father was one of these children. Later, when four small offspring sat around his table, he initiated the same practice. (As far as I know, his brothers and sisters have done similarly in their homes.) We never discussed whether or not we wanted to do this; it was just always done and never, to my knowledge, questioned. Reading material was chosen according to our ages. Often at the evening meal we read from a Bible story book, but at least once a day we read short selections from the Bible. For some reason we read Proverbs more than any other single book; my parents must have believed that book contained an extraordinary amount of wisdom for every-day living.

To the children in our family this was a logical thing for a Christian family to do. No one left the table, unless for special reasons, until we read the Scriptures togeth-er. This was no legalistic ritual; it was family habit. Thinking back, I remember numerous instances when our friends called for us and we asked them to wait until we had finished dinner. Dessert may have been served, but none of us ever considered the meal finished until we had read together.

Gladys Hunt

Gladys Hunt, *Honey for a Child's Heart* (Zondervan Publishing House, © 1969), pp. 89-90. Used by permission.

Mrs. Gladys Hunt

Author of *MS Means Myself, Honey for a Child's Heart, Does Anyone Here Know God?* and others

Mrs. David (Karen) Mains

Author of *Open Heart, Open Home*
Wife of pastor of "Chapel of the Air"

One tradition that marks the David Mains family clan is an insistence on evaluation. We rarely attend any media function or performance, whether it be a concert, the theatre or just an evening of television, without asking ourselves and the children to rate the experience. David invariably asks, "Well, how do you rate it? What number do you give it, from one to ten?"

The purpose of all this is not to raise snobbish critics, but to develop a healthy sense of evaluation in ourselves as well as the children in order that we and they may not be helpless in the face of the incredible media bombardment of the secular generation.

Once we have given our number rating, we share together the reasons why we have picked 3 or 7 or 10. At this point much discussion ensues which encourages the idea process in grade schoolers as well as teens. We want the children to know why they have attended certain functions or why not. What was the value of specific events, or why was it valueless? What were the Christian themes, or which were anti-God? What were the worldviews of the directors, creators, and participants?

The children are learning that Christian thinking demands a Christian philosophy of viewing. There are some (really, many) events we deny ourselves because of that developing philosophy. They are either too banal to deserve our time or too tawdry to involve our spirits. We feel that Christians must learn to evaluate what they see, and we feel that we are giving the children a tool that will protect them against this media world. They are developing spiritual defenses and are learning to approve the excellent and to recognize what is honorable, just, pure, lovely, gracious, or worthy of praise.

Karen Mains

Mrs. Pat (Dede) Robertson

Author of *My God Will Supply*
Wife of founder of Christian Broadcasting Network
and host of "700 Club"

Christmas Eve at the Robertsons' centers around the birth of our Savior, Jesus. There is a lovely old crèche (a manger scene) which was given to me by my aunt and uncle the year I discovered there was no Santa Claus. The stable is made of window shade rollers and slats (their business enterprise). The figures are made of delicately painted German porcelain. All have survived many moves and even a fire with only a few lost sheep and some broken heads which were easily repaired with Elmer's Glue.

Dressing the house in its Christmas finery is a family thing with the boys cutting the green boughs and holly, and Pat often joining in on the search for the perfect tree, its cutting, and final stand. The manger scene is set up without the baby Jesus, and all lies in readiness for Christmas Eve. After a traditional supper (traditional since living in Tidewater, Virginia) of scalloped oysters, chicken salad, hot ham biscuits, cranberry orange ring, and orange date nut bread, we gather around the piano singing Christmas carols and sharing with one another. Soon Pat picks up a Bible or has one of the children bring him one. This is the signal for us all to gather around him at the crèche.

Turning to Luke 2, Pat reads that beautiful account of the very first Christmas—the birth of our Savior, Jesus Christ. The children are encouraged to share what this means to them. Pat leads us all in a prayer of thanksgiving for God's love and God's willing sacrifice of His precious son for each one of us.

Then—the big moment—the youngest child, who knows where He is hidden, has the privilege of placing the baby Jesus in the manger. The first to do this was Tim, who quickly surrendered to Gordon, who later surrendered to Ann, who is carrying on the tradition until a grandchild appears on the scene.

What a joy to watch the little ones' eyes light up and to see the tender care that is given to the proper placement of the tiny figurine; to see the bright shining eyes of the others as they watch breathlessly to make sure it is properly done. A tradition, yes, even a ritual, but one which has helped to instill the all-encompassing love of God for each one.

Sincerely,

Dede Robertson

Mrs. Michael (Donna) Nason

Author of *Tara, Child of Hopes and Dreams*, and
co-author with husband of *Robert Schuller: The Inside Story*.

The most meaningful part of our day is always bedtime. I strive to make it as unhurried as I possibly can, a time of tranquility bathed in love. There is something about those sweet smelling, freshly scrubbed little bodies clad in pajamas that is simply irresistible. My own mother always held bedtime sacred and "tucked me in" each night until I left home to marry. Now I know the joy of my own little ones' nightly call, "Mommy, will you please tuck us in?"

We generally read a story, one that they have picked out. It may be a Bible story or Dr. Seuss or Shannon's favorite for over a year now—Superman. Now that Christa is learning to read, she always reads several pages out loud from an appropriate book of her choice.

This is a time with no interruptions, when the children have my undivided attention. It often becomes a "talk it over" time, a time for secrets and confidences. And I always conclude with prayer. I pray for each child individually and specifically, asking that their needs for the moment be met. And I praise God for His mercy and for His love, for His sacrifice for us, and for the wonderful plan He has for each child's life. And I ask Him to guard our home all through the night and to keep us all safe and healthy. The children's prayers come next. Sometimes they are no more than the familiar "Now I lay me down to sleep." But at times they are hauntingly poignant such as Tara's (she is quadriplegic as a result of brain injury suffered at age 2) "Please help me to walk,

God, so I can walk to your house." Our Mark, always the clown, surprised me one night at age three and a half when he prayed, "Now I lay me down to sleep. I close my eyes, I go to sleep, I wet the bed."

About the time I have turned out the light and am ready to make my getaway, the most angelic little voice invariably asks, "Mommy, will you sing me a song?" And I'll sing a quick chorus of "Jesus Loves Me" or "Cum Bah Ya." Then, just as I am settling down on the couch in the family room, the patter of little feet can be heard accompanied by that desperate cry, "I gotta go potty!" or perhaps "I need a dwink-a-water!" And with that final dash into neutral territory, the troops are down for the night.

Donna Nason

Mrs. Ted (Dorothy) Engstrom

Wife of President of World Vision

We talked to our three children and we have come up with the following list of special memories.

The last day of school in Wheaton, Illinois (while Ted was President of Youth For Christ) I would pick up the children at school and head for Michigan, station wagon packed including our darling black shaggy dog, Muggs. After driving 150 miles we arrived at Maranatha, Muskegon, Michigan.

At the entrance the boys always let Muggs out so she could race us to the cottage. She always beat us and was always on the top step waiting for us.

We all spent summers at the Maranatha Bible Conference, working, painting, playing and learning together. Many pictures flash into our minds of camp life together.

For instance, the kids and I covered all the ceilings with egg carton separators. Then with the left-over cartons they built a tree house and decorated a cave.

We had hung a pink frying pan from a tree limb. We used this as a gong to sound our dinner call, and the kids could hear it all the way down the beach.

One year the boys found an old rowboat with the front end crushed. They named it Sunken Sam. Gordon piled cement slabs in the rear end so the front end with the hole would ride well out of the water. It was quite a sight watching them (Muggs, too) paddling down the channel.

Maranatha made a great impact on the lives of our three children. It's fun to hear them talking, even yet, about those days.

Dorothy

Mrs. Rex (Maude Aimee) Humbard

Wife of world-famous evangelist and pastor of
The Cathedral of Tommorrow

One of our rarest and most unusual family traditions is the one that Rex and I have with our wedding anniversary. We have celebrated our August 2, 1942 wedding anniversary more than 450 times.

We observe it, not just once a year, but on the second day of every month. That has not always been easy to do, but in spite of all sorts of circumstances, we have not missed one of these monthly anniversaries yet.

Having an unusual tradition about our wedding anniversary seems only the right thing to do because our wedding was rather unusual. We were married just before the congregation was dismissed at the end of a church service at Cadle Tabernacle in Indianapolis, Indiana. The original Humbard family had been holding an evangelistic campaign there and the huge building was packed. I took my place immediately as one of the Humbard family members and sang in the service the very next night.

From there, the Humbard family went to Mishawaka, Indiana, for the next evangelistic campaign. While they were there, we celebrated our one-month anniversary. To commemorate it, Rex gave me a white lace dress with maroon velvet along the bottom. I wore it in the service on our one-month anniversary night.

The second month, Rex gave me a set of silverware. The next month, it was a diamond dinner ring, then a wristwatch, and so on. Every month it has been a card, or a gift, or a dinner out, or something special or unusual.

Each of us plots and schemes to find ways to help trick or beat the other every month in saying "Happy Anniversary." Many times both of us have stayed awake, but pretended to be asleep, waiting for the clock to pass midnight trying to be first to say, "Happy Anniversary."

On one of those monthly anniversaries Rex was in Australia to hold a rally. I had stayed at home, being too ill to travel. Rex placed a person-to-person overseas telephone call to me. I accused him of being a great big sneak because when the operator asked me if I was Mrs. Humbard, Rex cut in and shouted, "Happy Anniversary."

It makes me so mad when he gets it out first, because, when he is first he "rubs it in" all month. I will admit, however, that I do the same thing when I win.

Probably our most trying and anxious anniversary was our thirty-sixth annual anniversary, August 2, 1978, and we had to spent it apart. We were in South America, and just a few days earlier, I had sustained a near fatal heart attack in Brasilia, Brazil. We had been having some of the greatest rallies of our entire ministry.

While my life hung in the balance in intensive care, Rex struggled with the decision whether to finish the tour or not. Doing so would mean leaving me in the hospital at Brasilia while he and the family went on to Santiago, Chile. But I told him, "Go on and hold that rally in Santiago! The Lord will be with me here." Rex was in Argentina on the way to Chile on our thirty-sixth anniversary morning. He called the hospital in Brasilia and saw to it that I was wished "Happy Anniversary," and my wish was also returned to him.

By the following month, everyone was back within the United States, and I was on the way to recovery. The monthly race to wish one another "Happy Anniversary" was on again.

It is a tested and tried family tradition that has kept a spark of romance and a lot of love in our family all these years, and the end is not yet.

Maude Aimee Humbard

Our family seemed to spend more than the average amount of time traveling. As missionaries, we kept in contact with all of our churches in Brazil, so had to travel almost every weekend. Once or twice a year we would visit another country in South America, not to mention the heavy travel schedule during furlough when we could cover the United States.

Even as our children grew older, they still enjoyed the way we celebrated the progress we made toward our destination each day. We sang a special song everytime we crossed a state line, international border, or even a bridge. The song was borrowed from a gospel radio program heard from some local station along the way. We punctuated the ending with cheers and the honking of the horn.

I will try to write the musical score and give you the words.

Dondeena

Mrs. Dondeena Caldwell

Missionary, speaker, author

Ruth Carter Stapleton

Speaker and author of *The Gift of Inner Healing* and *The Experience of Inner Healing*.

When we grew up as children, we as a family group lived in the country. Jimmie was the oldest and responsible for the younger children and he created a playground for us because we were too poor to have our own toys. He made for us a wooden ferris wheel and saddled the horses for us younger kids, and we played together and had more fun; but it was Jimmie who was responsible for creating the family closeness and togetherness.

Rosalynn was always a part of the family as we grew up together and we considered her a sister. As we grew up there came to be quite a bit of age difference between us, and at the age of sixteen there was a period of time we were all scattered in our own directions. Not until Jimmie's first political campaign did we, again, begin to have family unity and togetherness. When Jimmie ran for office, that was the real beginning of family security.

There are so many things that go into making up a family and family traditions. Of primary importance is the way a family cares for one another. There must be a oneness and a real belonging—a sense of possessiveness and of being possessed by the group one calls "family." This becomes a reality only when mother and daddy are in love with each other and with their children. There have been families where the children, having been brought up in the same surroundings, formed a completely different family group of their own with differing goals and ways of life and living far from their brothers and sisters. If parents show the love and worth of their children to them in ways that are meaningful and helpful and when needed, the family itself becomes a tradition.

Church and Sunday school attendance are traditional for many families, but, again, it has to be important for mother and dad as well as for the children. Special occasion picnics, fishing trips, camping, and nature study are all tradition-building events if a family holiday is built into them. It is most essential for the parents to want to build traditions and then naturally to introduce their desires to the family in ways that make them important enough to be carried forward to other generations.

Yours in Christ,

Ruth Stapleton

Ruth Stapleton

Mary C. Crowley

Founder of Home Interiors & Gifts, Inc., Dallas, TX

When we built the home where we have lived the past eight years, there was a little piece of wooded land across a creek that was attached to our property. On this we built a Family Chapel. It has become a very special place and was built with the idea in mind for the family to have a quiet place to come apart. Because we are in business, we have many calls and much demand on our time and attention.

At Thanksgiving, Christmas, and other comings-together, we go to the Chapel. Each member of the family, each grandchild, son, daughter, or nephew, or whoever might be with us at that time, tells of something for which they are especially grateful, and each one has a special prayer time—each one prays.

At Christmas we often have each person tell me in advance their favorite dish which they would like to have for Christmas dinner, and their favorite verse that has sustained them during the past year. Then I prepare the special dish and we read the favorite verses around the table. We pray for one another, and especially that they will be kept in God's will and in His care.

When our children were very little, we were in the midst of war, money was very scarce, there were no daddies anywhere, and each mother had to work hard to build the family traditions for her little brood. (I think this is true today with so many single family heads.) I would take a single dip of ice cream and put sugar

cubes soaked in lemon extract on the top, light the sugar cubes, turn out the lights, and we would have "a party." Many were the times the kids would say when it was burned out, "Light it again, Mama; light it again!" This would give an opportunity to talk to them about the real light of the world—Jesus Christ.

Right now we have four teenagers in college, and they tell me it means a great deal for each one to know that they are being prayed for daily, and that when they come home for a weekend and come to grandmother's house, there will be special dishes prepared just for them. People say I cook with love and butter—I guess that's true.

My prayer and hope, of course, is that this will extend to them as they build their own families. We encourage all the families with whom we come in contact in our business to enrich their lives with memories of their own, and especially if they do not come from a family with traditions, they can start their own, even in their young life. There is something about a family tradition that carries one through when one might be far away, or lonely, or tempted to go astray from family teachings.

Mary C. Crowley

Kathi Lee Johnson

Recording artist, guest host on "Good Morning, America," and television feature reporter

In the early 1960s a doctor suggested that we spend several weeks at the seashore to alleviate some of my sister's asthmatic symptoms. My parents immediately drove to Rehoboth Beach, Delaware to find an ocean apartment to rent during the coming summer season. While scouting the town, Mom found a charming "gingerbread" house nestled in the pines, but my father noticed a dilapidated old Victorian boarding house with a "for sale" sign hanging precariously on the side of one of its weathered shingles. Ignoring my mother's protests, he asked the realtor to show him the property, only to discover that the exterior was "House Beautiful" compared to the sight before them as they stepped inside. As they rummaged through the forty rooms and eight bathrooms of filth, rotted debris, graffiti, and dead birds, my mother threatened to divorce my father if he took one more step. But, true to form, he kept right on trudging through the mess even discovering a wonderful secret stairway to the gabled attic!

After purchasing the "Rehoboth Inn," the five of us began our weekend treks during the bitter winter months armed only with small room heaters, buckets of cleaning paraphernalia, paint, and lots of courage. As a family we have been making the same excursion for fifteen years, watching a lonely old weather-beaten inn take on new life. Of course we children were thrilled to pieces about

the project and even Mom, courageously battling the mounds of dirt, forgave my father as each new room we tackled took on cleanliness and character.

Today, "Rehoboth Inn," shining, clean, and inviting, functions as a Christian retreat center and beach evangelistic headquarters. But, in a very personal way, it stands as a testimony to the hard work, togetherness, and tenacity of a not so "traditional" family that believed, and still believes, that the value of ownership is only realized through the pride of equally valuable earnership.

Kathie Lee

Mrs. Strom (Nancy) Thurmond

Wife of South Carolina Senator

We have many family rituals which "we reenact" each year, but perhaps my most favorite is at Christmas time. For many years, our children reenacted the nativity scene—complete with shepherd staffs and, of course, we always had a baby to be "the Christ child." Now that our children are older, however, we have had them memorize Scripture and have had them build nativity scenes, both disposable and permanent.

Also, each year we learn new Christmas carols, and by now we have a complete memorabilia of joyous Christmas strains to share with those less fortunate and our neighbors.

In the kitchen, we always try to do individualized cookies, a gingerbread house, which is given each year to the children's hospital, and, also, a plum pudding filled with lucky coins.

As to Christmas crafts, our children spend many, many weeks making their own gifts to give to others. They have made candles with a cardboard backing, which says "Jesus is the light of the world," wreaths made of nuts and natural trimmings, and Christmas trees made of pine cones and glued glitter.

In all of these crafts, our one objective has been to have the children give something of themselves to others and to deemphasize the material aspects of Christmas.

Of course, I could go on and on, but this gives you just a hint of some of our happiest memories from Christmas each year as we try to mold and nurture our children to think of Christmas as a celebration of Christ's birth and an opportunity through the gift of the Saviour to give hope and joy to others in the years ahead.

Nancy

Nancy Thurmond

Mrs. Bill (Vonette) Bright

Wife of Campus Crusade for Christ Founder and President

Practicing Motherhood with a Busy Schedule:

I tried to schedule nothing but family activities before or after the children returned from school. I personally picked them up from school rather than assigning someone else to drive them home. This was the time of day that they wanted to talk. If someone else had to drive them home, I would try to be available when they returned with milk and cookies, or some sort of surprise.

I didn't make the children wait for answers or adjust to my schedule any more than was absolutely necessary. When we had guests and one of the children walked into the room, I taught them not to interrupt the conversation. As soon as possible, however, I stopped the conversation to meet the child's need rather than making him adjust to company. In no way did I want the boys to feel second to our ministry.

Probably the greatest tradition in our family has been family devotions. Nightly we have gathered as a family for Bible reading, prayer, and many family discussions. Whenever Bill was away, he tried to arrange his telephone calls to the office (our home phone connects to the same switchboard) when we would be together,

usually just before bedtime. We prayed together as a family even over the phone. For overseas calls, of course, our prayers were very brief! We found this devotional time extremely important. Praying together was a help in keeping communication lines clear and we learned to pray for God's will in our lives—not just what father, mother, and the children wanted. Now that the children are grown, I think this is one of the traditions they appreciate most.

Vonette

Mrs. John (Sandi Patti) Helvering

Contemporary Christian vocalist

Many of my childhood memories came from the time my family lived in Phoenix, Arizona. My dad was the minister of music at our church which kept him very busy—except for Saturdays. Saturday was always the family day, and I can remember every Saturday waking up very early and piling in the car with Mom, Dad, and my two brothers and off we went to the desert for breakfast! Yes, breakfast. Dad would bring eggs, bacon, potatoes, bread, coffee, skillet, and anything else you might need for breakfast on the desert. Once we got there, Dad wouldn't let any of us, including Mom, do anything. He built a fire, and cooked the entire breakfast. He built a fire, fried the eggs, bacon, and potatoes, and we had a feast. My dad was pretty special, and ya' know what? I think breakfast is still my favorite meal!

Sandi Patti

Here are a few things that have been special in our home:

We begin the day together with a well balanced meal along with prayer and some spiritual food. We also conclude the day with prayer and the day's activities are shared. This is done as a family or on an individual basis depending on time schedules.

We emphasize birthdays with the favorite family dinner and gift giving with a cake and ice cream dessert. Friends and family are quite often included in this celebration.

Gift giving is minimized at Christmas time in order to focus our thoughts on the Lord Jesus Christ.

We try to attend, as a family, such activities as Little League games, musicals, school open house, school ball games, recitals, etc. To teach mutual interest in one another is a priority in our home. My husband's conviction in regard to this principle is evident by his frequently setting aside of pressing responsibilities in order to be with his family.

My best regards,

Pat

Mrs. John (Pat) MacArthur

Wife of Pastor of Grace Community Church, Sun Valley, CA and author of *The Ultimate Priority* and *Jesus' Pattern of Prayer*.

RESOURCES FOR FAMILY READING AND ACTIVITIES

Especially for Parents

Hunt, Gladys. *Honey for a Child's Heart.* Grand Rapids: Zondervan, 1969. A Christian parent and author directs teachers and parents to the best in books, not just those labeled as Christian, but all good books that are "honey for a child's heart." Contains a useful bibliography.

Larrick, Nancy. *A Parent's Guide to Children's Reading,* 4th ed. rev. New York: Doubleday, 1975. An inexhaustible sourcebook in paperback; includes materials for children of all ages, reading levels, and interests.

Dobson, James C. *Hide or Seek.* Old Tappan, NJ: Fleming H. Revell, 1974. Ten strategies for combating the false value systems of our society and for cultivating self-esteem, rather than inferiority, in our children.

Greer, Arthur E. *No Grown-Ups in Heaven.* New York: Dutton, Hawthorne Books, 1977. Based on Jesus' statement that one must receive the Kingdom of God as a little child, this book is a "Primer in Transactional Analysis for Christians (and Others)." The author tries to clarify the Christian gospel in light of T.A.

Kelly, Marguerite, and Parsons, Ella S. *The Mother's Almanac.* Garden City, NY: Doubleday, 1975. A comprehensive guide for loving and living with small children told from a mother's point of view. Here's a witty, practical approach to motherhood ranging from recipes for homemade baby food to camping out with kindergartners.

Sullivan, S. Adams. *The Father's Almanac.* Garden City, NY: Doubleday, 1980. An absolutely practical resource for fathers including everything from how to be a good expectant father to hobo recipes for father-child campouts.

Lewis, Margie M., and Lewis, Gregg. *The Hurting Parent.* Grand Rapids: Zondervan, 1980. A mother and son discuss isolation, fellowship, rejection, acceptance, anger, guilt, unconditional love, despair, hope, and forgiveness.

Gibben, Trish. *Pajamas Don't Matter (or: What Your Baby Really Needs).* Sacramento, CA: Jalmar Press, Inc., 1980. A delightful picture-word book for parents on what your baby really needs.

Leach, Joan, and St. Louis, Patricia. *Caring for Babies.* Cincinnati: Standard Publishing, 1978. A book on how to share God's love with very little people. For parents and church workers.

Schaeffer, Edith. *What Is a Family?* Old Tappan, NJ: Fleming H. Revell, 1982. A common-sense book about what God intends a family to be and why He made plans for it to be the basic unit of society.

Shedd, Charlie W. *Smart Dads I Know.* New York: Avon Books, 1978. All families have problems to be solved. Each of these dads found a unique solution to help his family work successfully as a unit.

Hern, Virginia, ed. *What They Did Right.* Wheaton, IL: Tyndale House. A "how-they-did-it" book. Accounts by many contemporary Christians of how their parents brought them up. These writers share the good and bad of their childhoods and honor their parents for "what they did right."

Benson, Bob. *Laughter in the Walls.* Nashville: John T. Benson Publishing Co., 1969. A collection of free verse about family living and personal being. You'll know better how to laugh at yourself, deal with daily family life, and know which moments to cherish!

Dobson, James. *The Strong-Willed Child.* Wheaton, IL: Tyndale House, 1978, Devoted to the unique needs of the strong-willed child, this thorough book focuses on infancy, childhood, and adolescence. A practical "how to" book on discipline.

Campbell, Ross, M.D. *How to Really Love Your Child.* Wheaton, IL: Victor Books, 1977. Most parents really do love their children, but do they know how to convey that love to them? Dr. Campbell discusses four crucial ways to relate love to our children.

Encyclopedia of Christian Parenting. Old Tappan, NJ: Revell, 1982. A comprehensive collection of advice on everything that relates to parenting: budgeting, vacationing, family worship, behavior problems, midlife crisis, communication, etc.

Dobson, James. *Dr. Dobson Answers Your Questions.* Wheaton, IL: Tyndale, 1982. Dr. James Dobson answers over 400 questions about marriage, child training, discipline, midlife crisis, depression, and many more topics in this comprehensive reference book.

Witmore, Nyla. *How to Reach the Ones You Love.* San Bernardino, CA: Here's Life Publishers, 1981. An unusually practical book taken from Nyla Witmore's experience with a style reminiscent of Erma Bombeck. She answers the question, "Why is it so hard to share my faith in Christ with the ones I love the most?" giving practical advice on how to reach them.

Rockness, Miriam Huffman. *A Time to Play: Reflections on Childhood and Creativity.* Grand Rapids: Zondervan, 1983. *A Time to Play* awakens, encourages, and stimulates parents to provide conditions and environments that will let their children be and become all their Creator intended.

Haystead, Wes. *Teaching Your Child About God: You Can't Begin Too Soon.* Ventura, CA: Regal Books, 1981. A practical scriptural guide on how to begin a young child's education in the Christian life.

Worship and Family Time

Haynes, Wanda. *My Book of Bible Stories. My Thank You Book. My Jesus Book.* Cincinnati: Standard Publishing Co., 1964 and 1963. Short stories or thoughts useful for family worship with very young children. Large, lovely, full-color pictures by Frances Hook to look at, too.

Lewis, C. S. *The Chronicles of Narnia.* New York: Collier-Macmillan Publishers, 1970. This set of great adventures with allegorical spiritual meanings is as much a "must" as *Pilgrim's Progress* is for adults. These are books to intrigue and involve the whole family. Great classics in Christian literature.

Haan, Sheri Dunham. *A Child's Book of Bible People.* Grand Rapids: Baker Book House. A super book for fun, painless, planned worship with young children. Poems, rhythm games, songs, and stories to *really* teach Bible stories.

Egermeier, Elsie E. *Egermeier's Bible Story Book.* Anderson, IN: Warner Press, 1969. For older children, clear up to college. Very well written, thorough, and accurate. The very best of its kind, and with questions and answers.

Vaughn, Ruth. *What's a Mother to Say?* Anderson, IN: Warner Press, 1981. A very special book that is a must for parents and teachers. Beautifully puts into words the cardinal doctrines so difficult to share meaningfully with those we love most, our children.

Bock, Lois, and Working, Miji. *Happiness Is a Family Time Together. Happiness Is a Walk with God.* Old Tappan, NJ: Fleming H. Revell, 1975 and 1977. Creative plans for fun-filled evenings of giving, sharing, loving, discovering, and learning more about each other and God.

Watson, Jean, ed. *The Pilgrim's Progress: In Modern English. The Princess and Curdie. The Princess and the Goblin.* The Family Library Series. Grand Rapids: Zondervan, 1980. Read-aloud alternatives to television for children 8 and older.

Vuilleumier, Marion. *Meditations by the Sea.* Nashville: Abingdon Press, 1980. Short devotions by one who lives by the sea, comparing the sea's horizon to the Christian's spiritual life—unfathomable, unlimited, full of secrets. Take this one on vacation at the oceanside, or use at home when your soul is dry.

Bloom, Marjorie. *Devotions for Your Family: Sharing in a Study of Mark.* Waco, TX: Word Books, 1978. Short devotions from Mark with questions and guided prayers especially for children, teenagers, and adults.

Blair, Caroline G. *Prayers for Mothers.* Valley Forge, PA: Judson Press, 1980. Refreshing pauses to help young mothers count their blessings and see God's love in daily life.

Hinton, Pat C. *Prayer After Nine Rainy Days and Other Family Prayers.* Minneapolis: Winston Press, 1978. Funny, tender, sunny, and rainy-day prayers for the living, breathing (sometimes hollering, fussing) family.

Ahrens, Herman C., Jr., ed. *Tune In.* New York: The Pilgrim Press, 1968. A poignant collection of poems, prayers, and ponderings about life, God, and the universe. Special appeal to young seekers.

Nouwen, Henri J. M. *With Open Hands.* Notre Dame, IN: Ave Maria Press, 1972. A beautiful book of poignant words and pictures about openhanded living.

Narramore, Clyde. *How to Begin and Improve Family Devotions.* Grand Rapids: Zondervan. A handbook on how to get started at family worship and how to make the experience valuable.

Frost, Gerhard E. *Blessed Is the Ordinary.* Minneapolis: Winston Press. Learning to accept each day as a gift from the Father's hand, we learn also to unwrap the hidden beauties in an ordinary day.

Marshall, Catherine. *God Loves You.* New York: McGraw-Hill. This small gift edition contains some of the warm, humorous stories Peter Marshall used in his famous children's sermons and in his family's prayer time.

Taylor, Kenneth N. *Devotions for the Children's Hour.* Chicago: Moody Press. Questions common to every child about God, creation, Jesus' life, and many other scriptural themes are answered in straightforward language.

Mattson, Ralph. *Mr. Sief.* Old Tappan, NJ: Fleming H. Revell Co. This book is an exciting innovation in children's (and grownups') books. Graphically it is great fun! The text makes each reader hauntingly aware that he is reading his own familiar autobiography.

Arch Books Aloud Series. St. Louis: Concordia Publishing House. Delightfully illustrated, inexpensive Bible stories in modern idiom. Some stories are available with records, so a child can read on his/her own.

Scanlan, Betsey, ed. *The Family Bible Study Book #1 and #2.* Old Tappan, NJ: Fleming H. Revell. An excellent way to study the Bible together as a family on a regular basis. Good for *any* Bible study group because it is easy to follow and understand.

Peale, Norman V. *Bible Stories.* New York: Jove Publications. A great way for the whole family to relate the Bible to real life. A delight to read.

Reilly, Terry, and Reilly, Mimi. *Family Nights Throughout the Year.* St. Meinrad, IN: Abbey Press, 1980. Active family times that help the whole family focus on God.

Jahsmann, Allan, and Simon, Martin P. *Little Visits with God* (series). St. Louis: Concordia Publishing House, 1957. Devotions for families with small children. Illustrated by Francis Hook.

Hook, Martha, and Boren, Tinka. *Little Ones Listen to God.* Grand Rapids: Zondervan, 1971. Thumbnail introductions to the Bible. Stories for very young children.

Hansel, Tim. *When I Relax I Feel Guilty.* Elgin, IL: David C. Cook Publishing Co., 1979. The aim of this book is to give you permission to give yourself permission to enjoy yourself more, to enjoy others more, and to enjoy God more than you ever imagined.

Blitchington, Evelyn. *The Family Devotions Idea Book.* Minneapolis: Bethany House Publishers, 1982. Includes good reasons to have family worship, what to incorporate, and what to do for all the age levels represented in your own family.

White, Mary. *Successful Family Devotions.* Colorado Springs, CO: NavPress, 1981. Practical help for making your family devotions an attention-holding, worshipful, and rewarding time for everyone.

Hymns for the Family of God. Nashville: Paragon Associates, Inc., 1976. A contemporary hymnal with a super selection of songs. Use it in your family devotions or worship time for singing traditional hymns of praise to God or contemporary, upbeat songs. Now available in paperback.

Keller, Phillip. *A Child's Look at the Twenty-Third Psalm.* New York: Doubleday, 1981. A beautiful description of the relationship between a shepherd and his flock and the parallels between that relationship and the one we have with our Shepherd—God. Written simply enough for children but profound enough for the whole family.

Taylor, Kenneth. *Stories for the Children's Hour.* Wheaton, IL: Moody Press, 1968. Ideal for devotions. Dr. Taylor shows your children the value of prayer, the true meaning of friendship, the importance of honesty, obedience, and kindness.

Books for Family Activities

List, Ilka Katherine. *Questions and Answers about Seashore Life.* New York: Four Winds Press. Take this book with you on your next vacation to the ocean. Great way to discover some of the marvels of creation.

Bock, Lois, and Working, Miji. *Happiness Is a Family Time Together. Happiness Is a Family Walk with God.* Old Tappan, NJ: Fleming H. Revell, 1975 and 1977. Creative plans for fun-filled evenings of giving, sharing, loving, discovering, and learning more about each other and God.

Skelsey, Alice, and Huckaby, Gloria. *Growing Up Green.* New York: Workman Publishing Co., 1973. Creating terrariums, arranging flowers, raising pumpkins. All kinds of gardening for family fun.

Rice, Wayne, et al. *Fun-N-Games.* Grand Rapids: Zondervan, 1977. Skill required for these games is the willingness to play.

Beetschen, Louis, ed. *You Can Make Country Treasures.* New York: Pinwheel Books. Translated from French, this small paperback has five delightful crafts to make from the wealth of the woods, fields, or parks. Great color photos!

Laverriere, Sophie. *You Can Make Tasty Treasures.* New York: Pinwheel Books. Another in the *You Can Make* series. Cantaloupe Martians, cookie castles, and watermelon walruses are just a few of the fun things a child can make with this colorfully illustrated paperback.

Cardozo, Peter. *The Whole Kids Catalogue.* New York: Bantam Books. A super catalog of every imaginable thing to do, make, and find. Includes many free things that can be ordered by mail.

Frank, Marjorie. *I Can Make a Rainbow.* Nashville: Incentive Publications, Inc., 1976. Every marvelous idea possible for making, creating, and doing at home and in the classroom. Covers many mediums. Really indispensable!

Cole, Ann et al. *I Saw a Purple Cow.* Boston: Little, Brown & Co., 1972. Recipes and instructions for more than 100 activities, from fun clay to puppet shows, to help little minds expand by *doing, doing, doing!*

Perry, Margaret. *Rainy Day Magic: The Art of Making Sunshine on a Rainy Day.* New York: M. Evans and Co., Inc., 1970. When there's nothing to do. Fun things to do with young children.

Wiseman, Ann. *Making Things: The Handbook of Creative Discovery,* Vols. 1 and 2. Boston: Little, Brown & Co. Great ideas for making things for kids, their friends, and the whole family.

Mack, Norman, ed. *Back to Basics.* Pleasantville, NY: Reader's Digest Press, 1981. All the how-to's for building and enjoying traditional American skills—everything from building a barn to constructing a solar water system.

Stein, Sandra Bonnett. *The Kids' Kitchen Takeover.* New York: Workman Press, 1975. A variety of kid-tested ideas for hours of pleasure in the kitchen and outdoors too.

MacKenzie, Joy. *The Big Book of Bible Crafts and Projects.* Nashville: Impact Books, 1981. Includes activities for teaching the Bible to children ages 4–12. Recommended for Vacation Bible School, Sunday school, nursery leaders, and parents. Includes 154 Bible-learning ideas for kids!

MacKenzie, Joy, and Bledsoe, Shirley. *The Big Book of Bible Games and Puzzles.* Grand Rapids: Impact Books. Bible games and puzzles for kids to enjoy with little or no assistance from grownup friends. Great learn-and-do stuff for travel, rainy day, or sick bed use. (Also a super way to entertain a "wiggler" in long adult-centered meetings.)

Forte, Imogene, and Frank, Marjorie. *Puddles and Wings and Grapevine Swings.* Nashville: Incentive Publishing Co., 1982. Things to make and do with nature's treasures for kids and their grownup friends.

Adventure Trip Guide. New York: Adventure Guide, Inc. A collection of 100 action-packed vacation ideas with information about what to expect and how to get there.

Simpson, Norman T., ed. *Country Inns and Back Roads, North America.* Stockbridge, MA: The Berkshire Traveller Press, 1982. A listing of very special, out-of-the-way places in the United States that still have charm and tranquility, including great family-award inns with home-cooked meals and quaint places to stay.

Farm, Ranch, and Countryside Guide. New York: Adventure Guide, Inc. A super guide to vacations that will let a family really experience life in the country or on a farm or ranch.

Wigginton, Eliot, ed. *Foxfire* series. New York: Anchor Press. What started as a study about the nearly-lost customs of early life in America and the mountain folk has become a series of intriguing handbooks on simple living and how to do everything.

The kitchen is a great place for family warmth and communication. Here is a list of books for cooking fun for kids and the whole family.

Betty Crocker's Cookbook for Boys and Girls. New York: Western Publishing Co., Inc., 1975. A bright, colorful, fun-filled book of things kids can really make with food.

Blanchet, Francoise, and Doornekamp, Rinke. *What to Do with a Potato. What to Do with an Egg. What to Do with Fruit. What to Do with Vegetables.* Barron's Cook Books, 1979–1981. Pictures books of nutritious food recipes for young children.

Laughlin, Ruth. *Natural Sweets and Treats.* Santa Barbara, CA: Woodbridge Press, 1975. Healthy treats for the sweet tooth. Over 300 recipes.

Young Children (to age 10)
Many of these titles are excellent for the whole family.

Williams, Margery. *The Velveteen Rabbit.* New York: Avon Books, 1982. The story of a stuffed toy told from the rabbit's point of view, with deep spiritual meanings.

Silverstein, Shel. *Where the Sidewalk Ends: Poems and Drawings.* New York: Harper & Row, 1974. Zany, crazy poems to tickle any kid's funny bone. Some with very serious points under all the giggles.

Silverstein, Shel. *The Giving Tree.* New York: Harper & Row, 1964. A parable about giving and taking; one of the single most meaningful books ever for children and for grownups.

Lionni, Leo. *Alexander the Wind-up Mouse.* New York: Pinwheel Books, 1969. Sure to provoke a discussion about being glad you are *you*.

Lionni, Leo. *Swimmy.* New York: Pinwheel Books, 1963. A story about how a smart little fish turned the oddity of being *different* into the blessing of being *special* by working closely together with others.

Lionni, Leo. *Frederick.* New York: Pinwheel Books, 1966. We are not all alike. We do not all do the same kind of work. Our world needs more than food and material things. Men (and mice) do not live by bread alone.

Lionni, Leo. *Tico.* New York: Pinwheel Books. Giving away outward treasures helps us to store up treasures on the inside. Real riches are kept where no one can see.

Douglas, Spencer, and Johnson, Ann D. *The Value of Respect. The Value of Believing in Yourself. The Value of Sharing. The Value of Responsibility.* Value Tale Series (Twenty-five titles in all). La Jolla, CA: Danbury Press, 1979. A series of books about famous people of history and science that teach values like respect, honesty, and responsibility.

Gruenberg, Sidonie, ed. *The Wonderful Story of How You Were Born.* New York: Doubleday, 1970. The wonder and beauty of the beginning of life are clearly explained and sensitively illustrated. Suitable for reading with a younger child or giving to older children to read themselves.

Why I'm Punished. *Self-Discipline. Inner Beauty. Tattletale. Old People. Life After Death. My Conscience. My Self-Image. Faults of Others and Me. Living and Dying. T.V. Cowboy. Love One Another.* Living Skills Books. Waco, TX: Creative Resources. A series of comic-book-size books for children, at only fifty-nine cents each, that teach important concepts.

Smaridge, Norah. *You Know Better Than That.* Nashville: Abingdon Press. Fourteen delightfully funny rhymes with rollicking drawings caution youngsters on the "dos and don'ts" of etiquette away from home.

Heide, Florence P. *You and Me.* St. Louis: Concordia Publishing House, 1975. God created each of us to be a unique, special individual. Isn't that wonderful?

Heide, Florence P. *God and Me.* St. Louis: Concordia Publishing House, 1975. Even though we can't see the sun at night, it is still there. We can't see God, but He is there, too.

Miyoshi, Sekiya. *The Oldest Story in the World.* Valley Forge, PA: Judson Press. The creation of the world retold in brilliant colors for children.

Fergus, Meryl. *Discovering Out of Doors. Discovering Little Things. Discovering Colors. Discovering at the Zoo. Discovering in God's World Series.* Glendale, CA: Regal Books. Superb color photos, sturdy covers, and large print make this series ideal for young children. Each book will stimulate more curiosity about the marvels of God's world. Scripture verses at the end of each book remind the reader who created the wonder of nature.

VanMeter, Harriet D. *Hands, Hands, Hands (Thank You God for Hands).* Richmond, VA: John Knox Press. Songs, poems, and photographs mix to make a book of charming surprises for very young children.

Poems of Childhood. Norwalk, CT: C. R. Bigson Co. The classics every child should have as a part of his/her heritage.

Dr. Seuss. *My Book About Me.* Westminster, MD: Beginner Publications, 1969. Helpful, simple, and delightful for building good self-images in young children.

Gaither, Bill, and Gaither, Gloria. *Especially for Children* Book Series. Gaither Music Co. Eight illustrated books with records (45 rpm), words, and music to learn while enjoying the songs of the Gaithers.

Gremmels, Marian Chapman. *The Cat Who Knew the Meaning of Christmas.* Minneapolis: Augsburg Publishing House. Do animals really talk during the stillness of the night on Christmas Eve? Lie awake with Andrew as he listens to his cat, Cricket. And hear some very exciting details about another winter night, that only cats who shared a stable could know.

Spier, Peter, il. *Noah's Ark.* New York: Doubleday, 1977. An award-winning book of intricate pictures that tell *without* words the story of Noah's Ark.

Joslin, Sesyle. *What Do You Say, Dear?* Reading, MA: Addison-Wesley Publishing Co., Inc., 1958. **Aliki.** *Keep Your Mouth Closed, Dear.* New York: Dial Press, 1966. Great fun for children (and for grownups who get to read them)!

Dobson, Danae. *Woof!* Waco, TX: Word Books, 1979. A book by James Dobson's 12-year-old daughter about two kids and a dog.

Kraus, Robert. *Leo the Late Bloomer.* New York: Windmill Books, Inc., 1971. Not all kids "bloom" at the same age, but patience and love will turn any hesitant bud into a lovely flower sooner or later.

Parkinson, Virginia. *The Manners Book.* Chippewa Falls, WI: Harvey House. Manners are simply being considerate of others. Firm rules to learn with Bible verses to support them. Great drawings. Our kids love this one!

Pottebaum, Gerard A. *Ninety-Nine Plus One.* Minneapolis: Augsburg Publishing House, 1971. The story of the ninety and nine with a *very* special twist for today's children.

The Lord Is My Shepherd. Kansas City, MO: Hallmark. Selected Bible verses beautifully and touchingly illustrated with this world-famous "poor child" by Betsy Clark. Makes a lovely gift.

Marxhausen, Joanne. *Three in One: Picture of God.* St. Louis: Concordia, 1973. Boldly illustrated comparison of the Trinity to the peel/flesh/core of an apple; meant to aid young minds in grasping the concept of the Godhead.

Marxhausen, Joanne. *If I Should Die, If I Should Live.* St. Louis: Concordia Publishing House, 1975. A beautifully simple book about forever life.

Tazewell, Charles. *The Littlest Angel.* Chicago: Children's Press, 1946. A moving Christmas story. Jesus accepts the most humble gifts, even those that may seem shabby compared to others, especially when they are given with love and adoration.

Hall, Adelaide. *The Wonderful Tree.* New York: Golden Press. This book provides a lovely experience with the seasons in God's world. All creation is a miracle of order and perfect harmony. Great illustrations.

Davis, Katherine. *The Little Drummer Boy.* New York: Macmillan Publishing Co., 1968. One of America's favorite Christmas songs forms the text of a beautifully illustrated children's book. Music is printed at the end of the book.

Marxhausen, Joanne. *If I Should Die, If I Should Live.* St. Louis: Concordia Publishing House, 1975. A beautifully simple book about forever life.

Pottebaum, Gerard. *The Festival of Art.* Minneapolis: Augsburg Publishing House, 1971. A very special retelling of the parable of the talents by an artist-father of his invitation for his children to create an expression of themselves from the raw materials he gives.

Marxhausen, Joanne. *Thank God for Circles.* Minneapolis: Augsburg Publishing House, 1980. Things have beginnings and endings—like lives. But God is forever—like a circle. We have a beginning—like a line. But when we get to the end of our line—there is a circle!

Zolotow, Charlotte. *The Hating Book.* New York: Harper & Row, 1969. The experience of feeling hated and hating in return is a poignant one for a child. Vibrant drawings.

Zolotow, Charlotte. *A Father Like That.* New York: Harper & Row, 1971. A touching story of the kind of father a little, fatherless boy wishes he had. Good for dads to read, too.

Zolotow, Charlotte. *If It Weren't for You.* New York: Harper & Row, 1966. Oh, to be the only child in the family! Life would be so grand—or would it? A humorous and honest portrait of living with a younger brother.

Brownstone, Cicily. *All Kinds of Mothers.* New York: David McKay. Mothers, just like children, come in different sizes with individual voices, abilities, and responsibilities. But they all have one thing in common—loving their children.

Travers, Pamela. *Mary Poppins.* New York: Harcourt, Brace & World, Inc., 1934. A classic in children's literature. Mary Poppins, with her blend of fantasy and nonsense, pervades this book which is at once poetry and fun and wisdom.

McGrady, Mike. *Jungle Doctors.* New York: J. B. Lippincott Co., 1962. A true story of men whose lives are built around compassion and dedication—jungle doctors—the men who bring medicine and hope to the wildernesses of the world.

Wilder, Laura Ingalls. *Little House Books.* New York: Harper & Row, 1935. The adventures of a family portraying a warm, loving home.

Alcott, Louisa May. *Little Women.* London: Octopub Books Ltd., 1980. The story of four New England sisters. Their day-to-day life, their quarrels, ambitions, and loves as they grow up are related at a rollicking pace, with warm understanding.

Farley, Walter. *Black Stallion.* New York: Random House, 1941. A beautiful story about a boy's love for his horse and the strange understanding that grows between them.

Wyss, Johann Rudolf. *The Swiss Family Robinson.* New York: Ace Books, 1980. A fun account of a family and their life on an uninhabited island. Obedience to parents and love for one's family are strong points the author makes.

Stevenson, Robert Louis. *Treasure Island.* New York: Ace Books, 1979. Always a favorite, especially with boys. Swiftly moving action from beginning to end. For the most part, the story is told in the first person by the boy hero, Jim Hawkins.

Spyri, Johanna. *Heidi.* New York: Western Publishing Co., 1977. The lovable story about a little girl, Heidi, who lives in the Swiss Alps with her grandfather. She is taken by her aunt to the city for school, but pines for her grandfather and the beauty and fresh air of the mountains, and is finally reunited with her grandfather.

Norton, Mary. *The Borrowers.* New York: Harcourt, Brace, Jovanovich, Inc., 1965. A classic children's story about some "miniature" people and the house they live in.

White, E. B. *Charlotte's Web.* New York: Harper & Row Publishers, 1952. The unforgettable story about the spider Charlotte who weaves messages in her webs to save the life of Wilbur the pig.

White, E. B. *Stuart Little.* New York: Harper & Row Publishers, 1945. An outstanding adventure about a mouse that goes voyaging. Great for boys especially.

White, E. B. *Trumpet of the Swan.* New York: Harper & Row Publishers, 1973. Louis, a swan born with the handicap of no voice, faces life with courage and a trumpet to win the love of his life.

Older Children, Teenagers, and Adults

Richardson, Arleta. *In Grandma's Attic.* Elgin, IL: David C. Cook Publishing Co., 1974. Every kid loves stories of "when you were young, Grandma!" Great experiences from days gone by with lessons that must be learned in *any* age.

Frank, Anne. *Anne Frank: Diary of a Young Girl.* New York: Pocket Books, 1981. The diary of a 14-year-old Jewish girl during the last year of her life before being arrested and killed in a Nazi prison camp.

ten Boom, Corrie. *The Hiding Place.* Old Tappan, NJ: Fleming H. Revell, 1974. The story of a Christian family's sacrifice to house and feed Jewish persons, their arrest and imprisonment, and the miraculous release of Corrie herself.

Zdenek, Marilee, and Champion, Marge. *God is a Verb!* Waco, TX: Word Books, 1974. Poetry and photographs depict the human expressions of praise and the need for divine help.

Leech, Bryan, and Sadler, Gwen. *It Must Have Been McNutt.* Glendale, CA: Regal Books. Who's to blame when something happens around your house? It must have been McNutt. Fun and inspiring.

Armstrong, William H. *Sounder.* New York: Harper & Row, 1969. This 1970 Newbery Medal Winner is a sensitive, moving novel about a sharecropper's family and their dog, Sounder, as they face the agonies of poverty and injustice with dignity.

Arnott, Anne. *The Secret Country of C. S. Lewis.* Grand Rapids: William B. Eerdmans. This biography of the fascinating man who wrote *The Chronicles of Narnia* traces his reluctant journey into the Christian faith from atheism.

Mattson, Ralph. *Mr. Slef.* Old Tappan, NJ: Fleming H. Revell Co. This book is an exciting innovation in children's (and grownup's) books. Graphically it is great fun! The text makes each reader hauntingly aware that he is reading his own familiar autobiography.

Hirschmann, Maria Ann. *Hansi, The Girl Who Left the Swastika. Hansi's New Life.* Wheaton, IL: Tyndale House, 1973. Two books by a former Nazi Youth Leader recounting her conversion to Jesus Christ from blind devotion to Hitler, and her adoption of America as her own new country.

Draper, Edythe. *Cool: How a Kid Should Live.* Wheaton, IL: Tyndale House. Daily selections from *The Living Bible* with black and white photographs and drawings. All in paperback, diary-fashion for the older child or young teen. Wonderful gift idea.

Maston, T. B., and Pinson, William M., Jr. *Right or Wrong.* Nashville: Broadman Press, 1971. Situation ethics are not limited to the adult world. Young people must make crucial decisions about drugs, recreation, and much more; and Christian youth must base their decisions on God's Word.

Christian comic books. Plainfield, NJ: Logos (several titles). Old Tappan, NJ: Fleming H. Revell (several titles). Great for kids who are going through the "I hate to read" stage. Comics with a purpose.

Herriot, James. *All Things Bright and Beautiful. All Things Wise and Wonderful. All Creatures Great and Small. The Lord God Made Them All.* New York: St. Martin's Press and Bantam Books, 1972–1982. The loving, joyful books by a Yorkshire veterinarian about his friends and neighbors both human and animal.

Klug, Ron. *Lord, I've Been Thinking: Prayer Thoughts for High School Boys.* Minneapolis: Augsburg Publishing House, 1978. Eighty-two prayers to help teen-age boys who are struggling to be honest with themselves and with God.

Sorenson, Stephen. *Growing Up Isn't Easy, Lord: Story Devotions for Boys.* Minneapolis: Augsburg Publishing House, 1979. Story devotions for growing boys (and girls) that show how God helps us meet all of life's challenges.

How Far Can I Go? *How Can I Be Real? How Can I Experience God? How Can I Fit In? How Can I Make Decisions? Answers for Youth* series. Grand Rapids: Zondervan. Biblical answers to questions young people deal with every day.

Paulus, Trina. *Hope for the Flowers.* New York: Paulist Press, 1972. A picture story for all ages about the risk and pain of becoming something special!

Eareckson, Joni, and Musser, Joe. *Joni.* Grand Rapids: Zondervan, 1980. The story of a young girl's struggle to wholeness as a quadriplegic. Inspiring for adults as well.

Lewis, C. S. *The Chronicles of Narnia.* Paperback set of seven books, boxed. New York: Collier-Macmillan Publishers, 1970. This set of great adventures with allegorical spiritual meanings is as much a "must" as *Pilgrim's Progress* is for adults. These are books to intrigue and involve the whole family. Great classics in Christian literature.

Nelson, Rosanne F. *Dear Jesus . . . I'm So Human.* New York: Doubleday. Candid letters to Jesus communicate the triumphs and defeats of a Christian striving to be more like Him.

Nutt, Grady. *Being Me.* Nashville: Broadman Press, 1971. These 90 pages probe the meaning of the statement, "I am a person of worth created in the image of God to relate and to live."

Holmes, Marjorie. *Nobody Else Will Listen.* New York: Doubleday, 1973. Prayers straight to God about the complexities of adolescent chemistry, from "terminal acne" to "romanticitis." He's really listening, too!

Narramore, Clyde. *Life and Love: A Christian View of Sex.* Grand Rapids: Zondervan. Direct, common-sense answers to questions young people ask about dating, marriage, and children.

Taylor, Kenneth N. *Almost Twelve.* Wheaton, IL: Tyndale House. For when it is time to talk about the facts of life. Handled very openly and sensitively. May be read with the child or read by parent and shared.

Shedd, Charlie W. *The Stork Is Dead.* Waco, TX: Word Books, 1976. Out of dialogue through correspondence with thousands of teenagers comes this frank, communicative approach to discussing sex.

Shedd, Charlie. *Letters to Karen.* Nashville: Abingdon Press, 1977. *Letters to Phillip.* Old Tappan, NJ: Fleming H. Revell, 1969. Letters about life, love, and marriage from a Christian father to his daughter (for girls) and his son (for boys). But for real understanding, read both books.

Leokum, Arkady. *Tell Me Why. More Tell Me Why.* New York: Grossett & Dunlap, 1969 and 1967. Four hundred answers to questions. A lifesaver!

Lanes, Selma G. *The Curiosity Book.* New York: Platt & Munk. Answers to the questions that young children ask: What makes lightning? Why does popcorn pop? Why don't all birds just stay south? What are freckles?

Wyse, Lois. *Small Poems for the Daughter I Love.* New York: Doubleday, 1972. Tender poems that will provoke tender talks about the daughter you love. (About age 12 and up.)

Wyse, Lois. *I'm Glad You Are My Son.* New York: Doubleday. A collection of word-gifts from a parent to a son.

Gardner, Richard A. *The Boys and Girls Book About Divorce.* New York: Bantam Books, 1971. A child psychiatrist wrote this paperback to help children of divorced parents adjust to their particular problems.

Lohmann, Hartwig. *I Can Tell You Anything, God.* Philadelphia: Fortress Press, 1978. A German pastor expresses moments of joy, sadness, tragedy, and reflection in prayers that speak to all young persons.

Dorothy Hamilton books. Scottsdale, PA: Herald Press. Great fiction with a moral impact. Especially interesting to boys: *Busboys at Big Bend, Tony Savala, Charco, Jason, Ken's Hideout,* and others. Especially interesting to girls: *Neva's Patchwork Pillow, Bittersweet Days, Mari's Mountain, Kerry, The Castle, Linda's Rain Tree* and others.

Lindbergh, Anne M. *Bring Me a Unicorn.* New York: New American Library, 1974. The diary of a young lady about her growing into a woman, her relationship at home, and her falling in love.

Maclay, Elise. *Green Winter: Celebrations of Old Age.* New York: Readers Digest, 1977. A priceless book of poems in celebration of old age. Every young person should thoughtfully read this to better understand that older people are only young people in older bodies.

Carson, Rachel. *The Sense of Wonder.* New York: Harper & Row, 1965. The famous author of *Silent Spring* gives children and adults a narrative (with fantastic photographs) to encourage awe in the mysteries of earth, sea, and sky.

Schaeffer, Francis. *How Should We Then Live?* Old Tappan, NJ: Fleming H. Revell, 1976. For Christians concerned about the direction secular humanism is taking our society. The author says: I believe people *are* as they *think.* The choices in the next decade will mold irrevocably the direction of our culture and the lives of our children.

Taylor, Paula. *The Kids Whole Kids' Future Catalog.* New York: Random House, 1982. This is a book of facts and photos about your future, plus lots of things to send for.

Holmes, Marjorie. *Two From Galilee.* Old Tappan, NJ: Fleming H. Revell, 1981. A sensitive novel about the young girl chosen to be the mother of the Messiah and her love affair with Joseph, God's plan for her, and life itself.

Lofts, Norah. *How Far to Bethlehem?* New York: Doubleday. A beautiful novel about the three kings whose thirsts and longings led them in search of the reason for their dreams.

Landorf, Joyce. *Joseph.* Old Tappan, NJ: Fleming H. Revell, 1980. A novel about the young man who was sold by his own brothers into slavery, yet obeyed his God in the most difficult times.

Landorf, Joyce. *I Came To Love You Late.* Old Tappan, NJ: Fleming H. Revell, 1977. An insightful novel about the two sisters from Bethany and their brother Lazarus whose home Jesus often called His own.

Eareckson, Joni, and Estes, Steve. *A Step Further.* Grand Rapids: Zondervan, 1980. The journal of becoming, from the author of *Joni.* Great for young people and adults as well.

Colson, Charles. *Life Sentence.* Old Tappan, NJ: Fleming H. Revell, 1981. The fascinating account of how Charles Colson, the "born again" believer, finds God drawing him back into prisons of every kind.

Sheldon, Charles. *In His Steps.* New York: Grossett & Dunlap. A time-honored classic on the adventure of walking "In His steps." A must for young people.

Lindbergh, Anne M. *The Unicorn and Other Poems.* New York: Random House, 1972. Lovely poems from a modern visionary.

Swanson, Donna. *Mind Song.* Nashville: The Upper Room, 1978. Unbearably beautiful poems from a pilgrim who dares to see.

Zdenek, Marilee. *Someone Special.* Waco, TX: Word Books, 1977. The tender words and feelings of the woman chosen to be the mother of the Messiah.

Welch, Reuben. *We Really Do Need Each Other. When You Run Out of Fantastic, Persevere.* Nashville: Impact Books. Two books from an author who seems to hear what we were afraid to say out loud.

Savary, Louis, and O'Connor, Thomas, eds. *The Heart Has Its Seasons.* New York: Regina Press. A collection of poems, writings, and photographs about humanity and its dreams.

Vanauken, Sheldon. *A Severe Mercy.* New York: Harper & Row, 1977. Recipient of Gold Medallion Award, here is a testimony to life lived at its deepest and of the conquering possibilities of faith and love.

Price, Eugenia. *Leave Your Self Alone.* Grand Rapids: Zondervan, 1979. Subtitled "The Paralysis of Analysis," this liberating book encourages us to do serious business with God and ourselves on the grounds of redemption and then to avoid the pitfall of damaging self-focus.

Dobson, James. *Preparing for Adolescence.* Ventura, CA: Vision House, 1978. Dr. James Dobson speaks frankly to adolescents about those most difficult teen years.

Bunyan, John. *The Pilgrim's Progress.* Grand Rapids: Zondervan, 1967. This classic is must reading for mature teenagers through adults. Its universality of spiritual appeal is unmatched.

Defoe, Daniel. *Robinson Crusoe.* New York: Bantam Books, 1981. A classic adventure/romance story about a young man who lives from one adventure to another.

Swift, Jonathan. *Gulliver's Travels.* New York: Doubleday, 1954. A political and social satire, aimed at the English people, but representing mankind in general, and at the English Whigs in particular.

Miller, Calvin. *The Singer Trilogy.* Downers Grove, IL: InterVarsity Press, 1980. Includes *The Singer, The Song,* and *The Finale:* three book-length lyric poems that make a poignant mythic retelling of the story of the New Testament.

Buscaglia, Leo. *The Fall of Freddy the Leaf.* New York: Charles B. Slack, Inc., 1982. Dist. Holt, Rinehart & Winston. For children who have experienced permanent loss and for the grownups who would like to help in finding a way to explain it.

L'Engle, Madeleine. *The Time Trilogy.* New York: Farrar, Strauss & Giroux, 1979. Includes *A Wrinkle in Time, A Wind in the Door,* and *A Swiftly Tilting Planet.* A wonderfully imaginative and exciting series of fiction that has become a young peoples' classic. No one should grow up without these books. (Newbery Medal Winner.)

L'Engle, Madeleine. *The Austin Family series.* Includes *Meet the Austins, The Young Unicorns, Arm of the Starfish.* New York: Farrar, Strauss & Giroux. Another series of fiction no teenager should be without. About a loving family of unique persons—warm and adventuresome.

Johnson, Lissa Halls. *Just Like Ice Cream.* Palm Springs, CA: Ronald N. Haynes Publishing, Inc., 1982. Especially helpful for pre-teens or teen-agers. A candid walk through a fictional story about a young girl who was lured into sex, became pregnant, adopted out the child, and through the pain of this traumatic experience became a Christian.

Clemens, Samuel L. *The Adventures of Huckleberry Finn.* New York: Dodd, Mead & Co., 1979. Huck is every boy who ever lived and also an individual worth knowing. This humorous novel of life on the Mississippi comes close to being America's most popular book.

Christian Living

Conway, Jim. *Men in Mid-Life Crisis.* Elgin, IL: David C. Cook Publishing Co., 1978. A book to help men cope with a difficult "passage."

Hart, Archibald D. *Feeling Free.* Old Tappan, NJ: Fleming H. Revell, 1979. Effective ways to make your emotions work for you as God intended them to.

Mains, Karen B. *Open Heart, Open Home.* Elgin, IL: David C. Cook Publishing Co. A book for the whole family who is committed to using hospitality as a statement of the lordship of Christ.

Marshall, Catherine. *Something More.* Old Tappan, NJ: Fleming H. Revell, 1976. *The Helper.* New York: Avon Books, 1979. Two books that will open new horizons of adventure in becoming, with the help of the Holy Spirit.

Putnam, Roy. *Life Is a Celebration.* Nashville: Impact Books. A book of release from the grip of depressive pessimism into the joy of God's incomparable energy.

Schaeffer, Edith. *A Way of Seeing.* Old Tappan, NJ: Fleming H. Revell, 1977. An invitation to see our own daily lives with a new perspective and a fresh vision.

Schaeffer, Francis A. *No Little People.* Downers Grove, IL: InterVarsity Press, 1974. Only Christianity, rightly understood and fearlessly applied, can solve the dilemmas of modern man.

O'Connor, Elizabeth. *Eighth Day of Creation.* Waco, TX: Word Books, 1971. An extremely helpful book about the Holy Spirit; God the creator at work within us, calling out our gifts and potential from the void of the universe within.

Schaeffer, Francis. *How Should We Then Live?* Old Tappan, NJ: Fleming H. Revell, 1976. For Christians concerned about the direction secular humanism is taking our society. The author says: I believe people *are* as they *think.* The choices in the next decade will mold irrevocably the direction of our culture and the lives of our children.

Benson, Bob. *Come Share the Being. Something's Going On Here.* Nashville: Impact Books, 1975 and 1977. Two books guaranteed to help you see with new eyes.

Kaufman, Barry N. *Son-Rise.* New York: Harper & Row, 1976. The touching true story of a young family's commitment to love and accept an autistic child. A real inspiration to any parent to go on loving through the tough times.

Massie, Robert, and Massie, Suzanne. *Journey.* New York: Alfred A. Knopf, 1975. The journal of two parents through the pilgrimage of daily life with a hemophiliac son. Chapters alternately written by father and mother. Sensitively revealing personal struggles and triumphs.

Zdenek, Marilee. *Splinters In My Pride.* Waco, TX: Word Books, 1979. Capturing the feelings so many of us have, Ms. Zdenek transforms them into valuable insights beautifully framed in lovely words.

Lindbergh, Anne M. *Gift from the Sea.* New York: Random House, 1978. A classic for women of all ages from a poet and lover of life who dares to search her most secret corners for her true self.

Powell, John. *Fully Human, Fully Alive.* Niles, IL: Argus, 1976. A book on positioning. All changes in the quality of a person's life must grow out of a change in his vision of reality.

Sproul, R. C. *If There Is a God, Why Are There Atheists?* Minneapolis: Bethany Fellowship, 1974. This book explains why some people say they are atheists, and why their position is without logical foundation.

Powell, John. *A Reason To Live, A Reason To Die.* Niles, IL: Argus, 1972. Coming to terms with tension, conflict, and anxieties, this book explores faith in its delicate balance of personal decision and personal surrender.

Powell, John. *Why Am I Afraid to Tell You Who I Am?* Niles, IL: Argus, 1969. Insights on self-awareness, personal growth, and interpersonal communication.

Sider, Ronald J. *Rich Christians In An Age of Hunger: A Biblical Study.* Downers Grove, IL: InterVarsity Press, 1977. A biblical case against hunger and an unforgettable discussion of the responsibility of the majority of American Christians in a time of world hunger.

Rifkin, Jeremy, and Howard, Ted. *The Emerging Order: God in the Age of Scarcity.* New York: Putnam, 1979. A stimulating discussion of the thinking committed Christian's potential role in the changing order if our culture is to be saved from its present course of decline.

À Kempis, Thomas. *The Imitation of Christ.* New York: Doubleday, 1976. The timeless classic by a simple monk whose intention is still valid to the modern reader: "of painting the way by which all would be able to follow Christ's teachings and by so doing to imitate His life."

Lawrence, Brother of the Resurrection. *The Practice of the Presence of God.* Translated by John J. Delaney. New York: Doubleday, 1977. This journal of one man's prayer life forces us to deal with the command of our Lord to "pray without ceasing."

Smith, Hannah W. *The Christian's Secret of a Happy Life.* Old Tappan, NJ: Fleming H. Revell. The time-tested classic written by an early American woman in search of wholeness in the Spirit.

Chambers, Oswald. *Daily Thoughts for Disciples.* Grand Rapids: Zondervan, 1976. A year's collection of devotions from the writing of Oswald Chambers, so soul-stirring they will trouble and inspire all day long.

Clarkson, Margaret. *They Also Sing His Praises.* Grand Rapids: Zondervan. Refreshing insights into God's Word. Nature-inspired by watching the birds which He created.

Sproul, R. C. *Objections Answered.* Glendale, CA: Gospel Light. A thoughtful book dealing with the hard questions Christians are most often asked by doubters. A must for college-age people.

Packer, J. I. *I Want To Be a Christian.* Wheaton, IL: Tyndale, 1977. A thinking person's discussion of what it really means and costs to be a Christian.

Sproul, R. C. *Knowing Scripture.* Downers Grove, IL: InterVarsity Press, 1977. Help for Christians who long to dig out the meaning of Scripture for themselves.

Keller, Phillip. *A Shepherd Looks at Psalm 23.* Grand Rapids: Zondervan, 1976. *A Gardener Looks at the Fruits of the Spirit.* Waco, TX: Word Books, 1979. Two books with unusual insight into the broader meanings behind some important spiritual similes.

Packer, J. I. *Knowing God.* Downers Grove, IL: InterVarsity Press, 1973. For persons who want to go beyond knowing *about* God to really, deeply knowing Him.

Trueblood, Elton. *A New Man for These Times. A Place to Stand.* New York: Harper & Row. Two classics on how to keep the vital balance between head and heart in a complicated and hungry world.

Getz, Gene. *The Measure of a Man: A Practical Guide to Christian Maturity.* Ventura,

CA: Regal Books, 1974. What the Bible says it takes to be a real man.

Getz, Gene. *The Measure of a Woman.* Ventura, CA: Regal Books, 1977. Wise words from the Scriptures to help women become what God wants them to be.

Landorf, Joyce. *Changepoints.* Old Tappan, NJ: Flemington H. Revell, 1981. Changepoints—the transition times. Sometimes you look forward to them, sometimes they come with a devastating shock. Joyce Landorf discusses how to navigate those changepoints.

Dobson, James. *Emotions: Can You Trust Them?* Ventura, CA: Regal Books, 1980. Practical guidelines and simple steps to help us understand, control, and channel our emotions.

Sine, Tom. *The Mustard Seed Conspiracy.* Waco, TX: Word Books, 1982. How Christians in America, with their churches, their time, creativity, and resources can make a world of difference by seeking the future of God in a world exploding with need.

Blitchington, Peter W. *The Christian Woman's Search for Self-Esteem.* Nashville: Thomas Nelson, 1982. The book focuses on two important dimensions of femininity—sexual nature and energy level, and discusses the problems common to women who attempt to satisfy both Christian and social standards in their search for recognition, approval, and a feeling of emotional and spiritual well-being.

Schaeffer, Edith. *The Tapestry.* Waco, TX: Word Books, 1981. The autobiography of Edith and Francis Schaeffer, encompassing six generations of family continuity and showing the fascinating interweaving of personal lives—threads—in the total fabric of God's world.

Gaither, Gloria. *Decisions.* Waco, TX: Word Books, 1982. A Christian approach to making the right choices. Help on making the decisions that daily bombard our lives.

Swindoll, Charles. *Improving Your Serve and Strengthening Your Grip.* Waco, TX: Word Books, 1981, 1982. Two fine books to encourage deepening and strengthening of a Christian's commitment.

Landorf, Joyce. *Irregular People.* Waco, TX: Word Books, 1983. Help for dealing with a difficult relationship with someone close to you; how to use spiritual resources for healing persistent hurts, becoming a reconciler, and avoiding becoming an "irregular person" in someone else's life.

Hart, Archibald. *Children and Divorce.* Waco, TX: Word Books, 1982. An authoritative, sensitive treatment of the crushing impact of divorce on children, and how to deal with that impact in the most compassionate, constructive way.

The Christian Marriage

Getz, Gene A. *The Measure of a Marriage.* Ventura, CA: Regal Books, 1980. Some common-sense help for enriching any marriage.

Sproul, R.C. *Discovering the Intimate Marriage.* Minneapolis: Bethany Fellowship, 1981. A practical guide to building a good marriage.

Timmons, Tim. *Maximum Marriage.* Old Tappan, NJ: Fleming H. Revell, 1977. Helpful real-life tonic for marriage, liberally seasoned with humor.

Timmons, Tim. *Maximum Living in a Pressure-Cooker World.* Waco, TX: Word Books, 1979. The title says exactly what this book is about. For anyone who lives in a world of stress (and who doesn't?) and wants to be God's person.

Dobson, James. *What Wives Wish Their Husbands Knew About Women.* Wheaton, IL: Tyndale Press, 1977. A priceless book for any man who wishes he could know what makes his wife tick.

Wyse, Lois. *Poems for the Very Married.* New York: Doubleday. Delightful poems that could only have been written to and by "the very married."

Larson, Roland, and Larson, Doris. *I Need To Have You Know Me.* Minneapolis: Winston Press, 1980. A practical workbook to work through together as a couple to help strengthen and enrich marriage.

Wheat, Ed, and Wheat, Gaye. *Intended for Pleasure.* Old Tappan, NJ: Fleming H. Revell, 1981. Sexual techniques and sexual fulfillment in Christian marriage.

Powell, John. *The Secret of Staying In Love.* Niles, IL: Argus, 1974. A book to help marriage partners understand themselves and each other better.

Shedd, Charlie, and Shedd, Martha. *How To Stay In Love.* New York: Ace Books, 1981. A book to help keep marriage alive, exciting, and filled with love.

Shedd, Charlie, and Shedd, Martha. *Celebration in the Bedroom.* Waco, TX: Word Books, 1979. A book to help Christian husbands and wives realize their dreams of an exciting and beautiful sexual relationship.

LaHaye, Tim, and LaHaye, Beverly. *The Act of Marriage.* Grand Rapids: Zondervan, 1976. How to achieve a mutually satisfying sexual relationship.

Landorf, Joyce. *His Stubborn Love.* Grand Rapids: Zondervan, 1971. Joyce Landorf portrays the reality of her broken marriage relationship and the answers she and her husband found for a joyful and healing resolution.

Wright, H. Norman. *Communication: Key to Your Marriage.* Ventura, CA: Regal Books, 1974. His ideas are ready to help you not just talk about communication, but to do it!

Wright, Norman. *Seasons of a Marriage.* Ventura, CA: Regal Books, 1974. Couples of all ages will discover the different stages of marriage that they will encounter, and how to prepare for the challenges they never thought about during their courtship period.

Dobson, James. *Straight Talk to Men and Their Wives.* Waco, TX: Word Books, 1980. Written to men, but intended for women as well, Dr. Dobson addresses a man's relationship to his wife and children; his work and money; his masculinity and emotions; his God and mortality.

Swindoll, Charles. *Starting Over.* Portland, OR: Multnomah Press. Healing for the broken past and fresh hope for the road ahead.

Wheat, Ed. *Love Life for Every Married Couple.* Grand Rapids: Zondervan, 1980. How to fall in love, stay in love, rekindle your love.

Swindoll, Charles. *Strike the Original Match.* Portland, OR: Multnomah Press, 1980. The things shared by Dr. Swindoll in this biblical book on marriage are realistic, believable, positive, nontechnical, and free from perfectionistic demands. Recognizing that the idea of marriage originated with God, Swindoll calls for a fresh and detailed look at God's original blueprint for marriage and the home.

Periodicals for the Christian Family

Adults

FOCUS ON THE FAMILY NEWSLETTER, 41 E. Foothill Blvd., Arcadia, CA 91006. This monthly publication by Dr. James Dobson's ministry, Focus on the Family, can be obtained free by writing the address provided.

THE CHRISTIAN HOME, 201 8th Ave. South, Nashville, TN 37202. Helpful guide for maintaining a Christian home.

MOODY MONTHLY, 820 North LaSalle, Chicago, IL 60610. A magazine for the whole family with provocative articles for adults and special sections for teen-agers and children.

FAMILY LIFE TODAY, Gospel Light, Glendale, CA. A useful and helpful little magazine filled with fun-time ideas, articles, worship helps, and advice for the family.

TODAY'S CHILD, 23033 N. Turkey Creek Rd., Morrison, CO 80465. Though aimed at teachers of children, this magazine of child evangelism and education is very helpful to the creative and informed parent.

MARRIAGE AND FAMILY LIVING, Abbey Press, 61 Hill Dr., St. Meinrad, IN 47577. A periodical aimed at enriching marriage and family life. Includes articles on adolescent problems, child rearing, family night plans, and marriage communication.

THE OTHER SIDE, 300 W. Apsley St., Philadelphia, PA 19144. A magazine dedicated to pursuing justice for the downtrodden of all nations and the Christian's response to need in a suffering world.

TODAY'S CHRISTIAN WOMAN, P.O. Box 1134, Dover, NJ 07801. Whether you are single or married, a career woman or homemaker, *TCW* is for you, today's Christian woman.

Young People

CAMPUS LIFE, Youth for Christ International, Box 2720, Boulder, CO 80321. Especially helpful to the teen-ager trying to be God's person in the school world.

HIS, InterVarsity Press, Urbana, IL. Published by InterVarsity Press, this is probably the best magazine available today for the thinking young person who is serious about being *His.* College and beyond.

SOJOURNERS, 1309 L St., N.W., Washington, DC 20005. A magazine dedicated to the belief that real Christianity is a revolutionary lifestyle in a materialistic world. College, graduate students, and beyond.

GROUP, Box 481, Loveland, CO 80537. A magazine full of articles and ideas for teen-agers, youth, and quest groups.

SOLO, Sisters, OR 97759. A magazine for single adults, dedicated to helping them be all God wants them to be, NOW!

CONTEMPORARY CHRISTIAN MUSIC, CCM Publications, P.O. Box 6300, Laguna Hills, CA 92653. For anyone interested in contemporary Christian music and recording artists. Contains information about new releases, top song and album charts, and interviews.

Special Products for Memory Making and Keeping

A red "You're Something Special" plate, handmade of fine ceramic. No two are exactly alike. See p. 87 for ideas of how to use this plate to say "we love you" at special times. To order write to: The Original Red Plate Company, P.O. Box 7965, Newport Beach, CA 92660.

Grandpa's Story or Grandma's Story, published by Wincraft Inc., Winona, MN: This keepsake and memories album for grandchildren is made for grandmas and grandpas to record all kinds of details about themselves and their lives, the interests and hobbies they enjoyed, the kinds of childhoods they had, the places they lived, the interests and hobbies they enjoyed, etc. The pages are actually envelopes in which grandparents can insert notes, letters, keepsakes, photographs, etc. This completed book makes a priceless gift for a grandchild. To order write to: Venture Management, 28 Ponco Trail, Kirkwood, MO 63122.

Grandparent's Family Book by Charlie and Martha Shedd: A put-together biography for grandparents to keep for their grandchildren. Contains places for information about the grandparents, the family, and the grandchild as he or she grows. To order write to: Doubleday & Company, Inc., 501 Franklin Ave., Garden City, NY 11530.

Grandparents' Book: Thoughts, Memories, and Hopes for a Grandchild by James Wagenvoord: A beautiful album and memories book for grandparents to compile as a grandchild grows, recording things such as notes and letters written, vacations shared with grandma and grandpa, talents demonstrated and special moments remembered. Like the other grandparents' books, this one would make a priceless gift to a grandchild when the child reaches adulthood (at high school graduation, on the wedding day, or as a farewell gift when entering the armed services or when leaving for college). To order write to: James Wagenvoord, 630 Third Ave., New York, NY 10017.

Memories by Bobb Biehl: This book may be given as a gift to parents or loved ones so that they can record their family history. Everyone over 30 should be recording his/her memories. It consists of 60 life-covering questions, each of which are supported by 3 to 10 additionally stimulating questions. To order write to: Classic Publications, P.O. Box 6128, Laguna Niguel, CA 92677.